NOT ONCE DID
His
PROMISES FAIL

NOT ONCE DID *His* PROMISES FAIL

MARVELLA L. MURRAY

*"I shall not die, but live, and declare the works of the Lord"
(Ps. 118:17, KJV).*

XULON PRESS

Xulon Press
2301 Lucien Way #415
Maitland, FL 32751
407.339.4217
www.xulonpress.com

xulon PRESS

© 2021 by MARVELLA L. MURRAY

All rights reserved solely by the author. The author guarantees all contents are original and do not infringe upon the legal rights of any other person or work. No part of this book may be reproduced in any form without the permission of the author.

Due to the changing nature of the Internet, if there are any web addresses, links, or URLs included in this manuscript, these may have been altered and may no longer be accessible. The views and opinions shared in this book belong solely to the author and do not necessarily reflect those of the publisher. The publisher therefore disclaims responsibility for the views or opinions expressed within the work.

Unless otherwise indicated, Scripture quotations taken from the New King James Version (NKJV). Copyright © 1982 by Thomas Nelson, Inc. Used by permission. All rights reserved.

Scripture quotations taken from the King James Version (KJV) – *public domain*.

Scripture quotations taken from the Holy Bible, New International Version (NIV). Copyright © 1973, 1978, 1984, 2011 by Biblica, Inc.™. Used by permission. All rights reserved.

Scripture quotations taken from the Holy Bible, New Living Translation (NLT). Copyright ©1996, 2004, 2007 by Tyndale House Foundation. Used by permission of Tyndale House Publishers, Inc.

Library of Congress Control Number: 2021-921760

Paperback ISBN-13: 978-1-66283-452-3
Dust Jacket ISBN-13: 978-1-66283-453-0
Ebook ISBN-13: 978-1-66283-454-7

Dedication

This book is dedicated to my husband, Wendell Murray, my gift from God, my soul mate and number one supporter; to my dear mother Ms. Iris who believed in me and gave me encouragement from the Bible; and in loving memory of my father Louis Lawrence who was a part of the miracle that gave me life.

Acknowledgment

First, I'd like to thank God for guiding me through a maze of health challenges, due to a brain aneurysm that could have been fatal, to share my story through this medium. It took ten years and some, and lots of encouragement from family, friends, and members of the community of faith, too numerous to mention here, for this book to materialize. The process was like a refiner's fire. BUT God! Revisiting and recounting the details of my journey, which began on October 8, 2011 *Not Once Did His Promises Fail!* BUT God! My husband, Wendell, Iris my mother, Maxine my sister, Marva my sister-in-law, Joanna (Pansy) my true and trusted friend from my teen years, Sis. Davidson "Sister D", family friend, Sis. Edwards "Sister Eddy" (now deceased), once my prayer partner, physical therapist Dr. Kadine, and her mother, Elder Icene, and all of whom provided me with details relating to my hospitalization that I had no recollection of. And to members of the North Bronx Seventh-day Adventist Church and other churches, including prayer teams locally and globally, to all I am indeed grateful.

To Brother Eric, my second pair of eyes and ears, and another set of fingers on the computer, thank you. And to the publisher and editors of this book, thank you for patiently working with me and taking a manuscript of mine and made it a reality. By giving me the opportunity to share my story with others. It is my intent that those who read this narrative will be inspired and led to believe that there's a God. A God who can make what seemed impossible, possible.

Table of Contents

1. The Genesis 1
   My Captivity 5
   Nothing Is Too Hard for God 10

2. United in Prayer 15
   Global Prayers 19

3. My Family Arriving in New York 25
   A Visit from an Angel and a Cryptic Message 32

4. Choosing a Rehab Facility and Transferred 41
   The Road to Recovery Begins 44

5. Home Sweet Home 63

6. Road to Recovery Continues at Home 69
   Fear or Faith 81
   Vertigo! Tinnitus 96

7. The Brook Began to Dry Up 103

8. Unexpected Changes 113
   Down and Out 120

9. Attitude of Gratitude, Thanks, and Praise 127
   Family, Friends, and Strangers 133

10. Reading to Understand............................. 147
    A Sound Mind 158

11. The Grim Reaper Strikes Twice 169

12. Make Me a Memorial and Lesson from Two Fruit Trees... 173

13. My Life Today....................................... 183

References 195

Introduction

This is my story—a story that is nothing short of a miracle that began on October 8, 2011. It was the day I suffered a cerebral aneurysm that changed my life forever. My motive for writing *Not Once Did His Promises Fail* was to take my readers on a journey to see how God shows His love for us in dark and depressing times and to help them see the results when we intercede in prayer for others, as well as to see how God uses people to intervene in our lives through myriads of ways we'll never understand. In this narrative, you'll see through Bible characters, scripture, religious songs, and educational readings, how God spared me from discouragement, despair, and a near miss with depression.

Throughout my experience, you'll see God's providential care and how He used my brokenness, pain, and suffering to heal me spiritually and physically. As you read this narrative, my hope is that you'll see God's love manifested in my life. And you'll see a God who relentlessly pursues us regardless of the trials we go through, a God who is faithful, loving and compassionate in all His ways.

For those of my readers who are struggling with your faith, as we all do at times, I hope that this book will inspire you. You'll take the time to acquaint yourselves with Jesus, and by doing so, you'll fall in love with Him. For those who have become hopeless, I hope, through the reading of my story, you'll find hope again. But most of all, I hope you'll fall in love again with a God who is madly in love with us. My readers, you have nothing to lose; neither do you have anything to fear, but much, much to gain. May you have a pleasurable read and your soul revived as you embark on this journey with me. Let's begin!

"For I know the thoughts that I think toward you, says the Lord, thoughts of peace, and not of evil. To give you a future and a hope" (Jer. 29:11, NKJV).

Chapter 1

THE GENESIS

I was looking forward to the long weekend, which included a national holiday to be celebrated on Monday, October 10, 2011. So I hurried home in the crisp fall air, and on reaching home, I began preparing for Sabbath. At sunset, my husband Wendell and I came together for our evening worship. We sang some Sabbath songs together to usher in the Sabbath, after which my husband proceeded to open up the Bible. Tucked away in the crevice of the first page of the Bible was a small, thin, rectangular piece of white paper. Written on the piece of paper was "For with God nothing will be impossible" (Luke 1:37, NKJV).

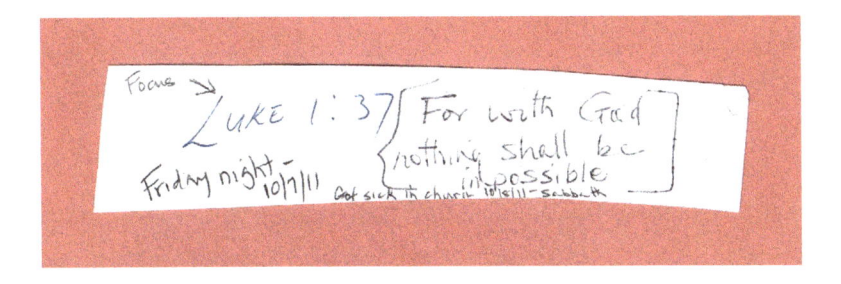

My husband showed it to me and the handwriting looked familiar; it was my own. It seemed that for some forgotten reason,

I'd written the verse on the paper and placed it in the Bible some time back. However, my husband decided to make this verse the focus of our worship. Looking back, I have asked myself the question time and time again, was this a premonition as to what was to transpire on Sabbath, October 8, 2011?

After worship that Friday evening, we both retired early to bed. We had a good night's rest. The next morning, we awoke bright and early. It was Sabbath, October 8, 2011, and I can recall it was a beautiful, crisp, sunny fall morning. The sun was shining in all her splendor. I remember telling my husband, Wendell, that morning that I just didn't feel like going to church. But within ten minutes of telling him so, I suddenly had a change of heart. It was the Lord's Sabbath; how could I not go to church to worship Him and fellowship with other believers? The Sabbath was a special gift to me from my Creator God. I had to make use of the gift. What was I thinking?

So I decided right then and there in our bedroom to go to church. I told my husband that I had changed my mind because if it was work, no matter the circumstances, I would have made every effort to go. So I got up from my comfortable bed, got ready, and we made our way to God's house of worship. It was the Sabbath. What better place to find ourselves, worshiping in the house of God with the other saints. This would eventually turn out to be one of the best decisions I'd ever made in my life. My life was spared. I was at the right place at the right time where I got the medical help I needed. Was this the Holy Spirit's doing?

Worship at our church always begins at 8:15 a.m. on Sabbath mornings with a program that goes by the name "Power Hour" and ends at 9:15 a.m. It is during this time that members within the community of believers unite in prayer, share their testimonies, and sing songs of praise to our Creator God. We were on time as usual for the first program of the day. It was customary for me to sometimes use the bathroom during this time on a Sabbath morning. At other times as one of the elected Sabbath School facilitators, I would spend the time either in the Sabbath School teacher's class, or I would be getting ready for the Sabbath School program when it was my turn to facilitate the Sabbath School.

However, on Sabbath, October 8, 2011, for some reason or by divine intervention, I was impressed with what was being said as each speaker stood and gave their individual testimony. I became an attentive listener that I didn't bother getting up from my usual seat. I didn't want to leave the sanctuary. I really loved what I was hearing.

"Fear not, for I am with you; Be not dismayed, for I am your God. I will strengthen you, Yes, I will help you, I will uphold you with My righteous right hand" (Isa. 41:10, NJKV).

My Captivity

I continued to sit and listened attentively. However, I became intrigued with the last speaker's comments. I raised my hand, as a signal to the individual leading out that I wanted to make a follow-up statement to what was said by the previous speaker. I can clearly recall standing and speaking. I began by going back and looking at the context in which God had given the promise to His people Israel. God allowed His people to go into Babylonian captivity for seventy years, and now He was telling them through the prophet Jeremiah He had plans, good thoughts, peace, and no evil toward them. He wasn't going to harm them. How could this be? I went on to parallel the children of Israel's captivity to the ones we experience in our personal lives today. I went on to say that our captivity today could be in the form of illness, finance, marital, or job-related, and we needed to be set free from these bondages.

Sometimes we are held captive for a very long time, as if there is no way out, *but* we have to rely on God to set us free. I reminded those present that the same God who allowed the children of Israel to go into captivity for seventy years was the same God we worship today. Despite the captivities we might find ourselves in, God still had great plans for us; He was still God.

After speaking, I took my seat in the corner of the pew in the aisle. As I sat there, suddenly I felt a hand, the size of a man's hand, with five distinct fingers, holding me over my right ear. I said to myself, "Who could be greeting me like this?" Next, I hastily looked around, but there was no one standing in the aisle. I found it quite puzzling, but the sensation of the hold over my ears still lingered. A few minutes passed, five minutes at most, and then I began feeling nauseous. I felt as if I was going to die and needed help. All I could do was to call out to Ivylyn a sister in Christ, who was sitting two pews behind me, and informed her that I wasn't feeling well.

She quickly came over to where I was sitting, and then informed my sister-in-law Marva, a registered nurse for many years, who was sitting in the middle aisle up front that I was complaining about not feeling well. Marva, hurriedly came over to see what was taking place. I told her that I wasn't feeling well. They both carted me off to the church's sick bay, situated in the front section of the church, next to the foyer, the elevator, and a flight of steps leading to the entrance of the church. The places I've mentioned would soon play a vital role in the beginning of my hospitalization. By then I'd become unresponsive and was surrounded by individuals from the medical profession, male and female. I was in good hands! With assistance from other medical personnel present that morning, I managed to get on the bed in the sick bay. It was then that I began throwing up what I had for breakfast that morning.

It was as if I was using my mouth as a paint brush and the floor as a piece of canvas to paint a picture. Purple stuff was flying all over the floor of the sick bay. This was the tell-tale sign of the smoothie I had for breakfast that Sabbath morning. The smoothie consisted of blueberries, strawberries, a ripe banana, and almond milk topped with flaxseed. The vomiting did not cease until I finally lost consciousness.

As told to me by my sister-in-law, Marva, it wasn't looking good. Vomiting wasn't a good sign. Present were individuals from the medical profession who with no reservation cleaned the mess I'd made on the floor. They didn't care that they were all dressed for worship. They rose to the occasion and chipped in. But the situation got graver. I needed to see a doctor fast. And it had to be very, very fast!

In the meantime my husband, Wendell, was in the Sabbath School teacher's class, unaware of what was happening. Marva his sister, went to get him and informed him as to what was going on. Without hesitation, he hurried to the sick bay. Just then Ladosha, another sister in Christ, on arriving to church, noticed a flurry of activities and inquired as to what was going on. As soon as she was told of the happenings, without hesitation, she took her cell phone out of her pocketbook and immediately called the emergency room at the hospital she had retired from some months earlier.

Shortly after, an ambulance with two emergency technicians arrived. In my unconscious state, I sensed that I was strapped into a chair, hoisted in the air, and carried out of the sick bay. I knew that I was taken on the church elevator because I felt when the chair I was strapped in made contact with the floor. As soon as the elevator doors reopened, I knew I was on the ground floor a little ways from the main entrance of the building. Next, I felt someone tugging at my right wrist. The person was trying to remove my watch. In my subconscious state, I managed to release the safety latch on the watch, removed it, and gave it to someone nearby. I knew I did this because I heard someone saying, "She removed her watch," and then I heard laughter.

Next, I was taken from the church building and to the waiting ambulance. As told to me, the technicians worked very hard trying to keep me alive. They kept talking to me but to no avail; the situation seemed to be spinning out of control. More help was needed. Time was of essence, and they were working against it. More and more it became grave. So, a call was made for another ambulance. At the arrival of the next ambulance, I was transferred to it. There, another trained technician took over and began tending to me. My condition was rapidly deteriorating.

By this time, the church broke out in a frenzy. There were people approaching the church building, who became curious on seeing two ambulances parked before the entrance of the church. Questions were asked. What was going on? Who was sick? Everyone—members, non-members and passers-by—wanted to know more. What was really going on? Curiosity was the order of the morning. How would this sudden drama play out?

"Ah, Lord God! Behold, thou hast made the heaven and the earth ... and there is nothing too hard for thee" (Jer. 32:17 KJV).

Nothing Is Too Hard for God

In the second ambulance, I was placed on a heart monitor and given oxygen. Whatever medication I needed at the time was administered by the technician. My sister-in-law Marva, a registered nurse, gave me this information. She was very supportive right through the ordeal and still is. Along with her professional knowledge, love, empathy and emotional support, I was in the right hands. God had placed me where I could receive the love and support I needed from people who really cared. But before the ambulance departed to the hospital, members of the prayer ministry group went into a season of prayer. I was told that they encircled the ambulance and stormed heaven on my behalf.

Waiting at the door of the emergency room for me was a team of doctors and nurses ready and rearing to go. They were waiting for me to arrive due to the call that was made approximately half hour before by my sister in Christ, Ladosha, who had just recently retired from the hospital. I was wheeled from the ambulance on a stretcher and quickly taken to a cubicle in the emergency room. There began a flurry of activities. The team had to work against the clock. A neurosurgeon was quickly called in, and then I was placed on a ventilator, and a CT scan was performed on my brain.

Some of the members of the prayer team rushed to the emergency room and quickly engaged in a prayer vigil. After offering prayers, they went back to the church building where prayer continued throughout the day in the sanctuary. My husband and his sister remained with me at the hospital, and according to my husband, it was around midday that he was able to return to the church building. He made his way to the sanctuary and gave the members, a progress report regarding my medical status. It wasn't looking good for me. Because I was still in the danger zone. So, he made the request for them to continue praying, and pray they did.

According to the surgeon's report, the CT scan that was performed showed that I'd suffered a subarachnoid hemorrhage—bleeding into the area around my brain. The bleeding was in the posterior fossa, compressing the brain stem. An angiogram was performed, and it showed that I'd an anterior inferior cerebellar artery (AICA) aneurysm (An aneurysm is a weak area in the wall of a blood vessel that causes the vessel to balloon and burst).

Before the surgery, a full anesthesia was administered followed by a cut in my skull. The incision ran from the back of my right ear, making its way down to the back of my head, where my head and neck kissed each other. The first surgery to stop the bleeding was unsuccessful. A large amount of blood still surrounded my brain. My entire neurological condition was rapidly deteriorating. Was that it? I was suspended between life and death. Sovereign God, was still in control. He had the final say in the matter. According to Wendell, the first surgery performed by the medical team was going to be the first and the last.

But not so fast! God wasn't finished with me yet. He was still on the case and stepped in just when I needed Him. He had a plan and a bigger purpose for my life. The neurosurgeon left the operating room, went to the waiting area where my husband and Marva his sister were. He explained to them in details what had taken place during the surgery. Suddenly the doctor asked my husband Wendell, "Do you have faith?" He quickly answered *yes*!

My husband knew what God's Word said about faith: "Now faith is the substance of things hoped for, the evidence of things not seen" (Heb. 11:1, KJV), and he believed it with his entire being. He'd been through many Red Sea moments in the past and experienced God's working in each situation. He knew without a shadow of a doubt that God would show up for him one more time. He was still going to take God at His Word because he knew that the God he served was "not a man that he should lie" (Num. 23:19, KJV). This was just another instance where his faith would be severely tested.

The doctor handed Wendell a piece of paper, had him sign it, and told him that he was going to make a second attempt. But before the doctor proceeded to make the second attempt, he outlined to my husband the post-surgery risks and benefits. The neurosurgeon told him that I could experience bleeding, infection, brain swelling that could result in further compression of the brain stem, and difficulty breathing. I could also end up in a vegetative state and experience problems with my blood pressure and heart rate that could lead to death. The odds were really stacked up against me. But my husband Wendell had strong faith in God. He was willing to exercise his faith and take the risk. Fear had to flee, and faith took its place. He knew that nothing was too hard for our God to do. Time was racing by, so he went ahead and quickly signed the consent form.

The second surgery began late the Saturday night and ended early Sunday morning. The second surgery was successful, but the next forty-eight hours were crucial. I wasn't yet out of the woods. Prayer was still needed. By this time my other half Wendell and Marva were feeling exhausted. After the surgery, at the advice of a member of the medical team, they went home. They both had been at the hospital since early Sabbath morning into early Sunday morning. It was time for a well-deserved break. They needed to get some sleep—if they could. The morning hours seemed longer than usual. No one knew what the outcome would be.

As time marched on, I was to learn that the child of God must wait on Him. For it's in times of waiting and stillness, God shows up and strength is born, "in quietness and confidence shall be their strength" (Isa. 30:15, NKJV). Going through this process, I realized that as I waited on Sovereign God, my relationship with Him became stronger. Waiting in patience became the order of the day for me. Day by day, I knew without a doubt that God was in control of my situation and I served an on-time God!

My husband reached home after 12 o'clock Sunday morning, feeling very tired and exhausted from the previous day's events. The next move he made was to get some well-deserved sleep. However, he didn't sleep for long. The season had caused a lot of leaves to accumulate in our backyard and so when he got up from his short rest, he immersed himself in raking and bagging the leaves. He had to get the bags ready for the next garbage collection day. As Marva told me, she had deep concern leaving her brother that Sunday morning all by himself. So, she telephoned, Elder Keith and Sister Andrea Williams who were also members of our faith and at the time, lived one block away from us. She called and asked them if they could assist. Shortly after, Elder Keith went over with breakfast and spent some time with my husband. It was later on in the day that my husband left for the hospital.

"It shall come to pass that before you they call, I will answer: And while they are still speaking, I will hear" (Isa. 65:24, NKJV).

Chapter 2

United in Prayer

From the onset the entire church community joined together and prayed earnestly about the situation. From the moment some members of the church arrived that fateful Sabbath morning and saw an ambulance parked in front of the church building and discovered what was happening, they immediately became engaged in intense prayer.

Prayer was also offered in small groups, in the divine worship hour, and in the evening's program. It was prayer all through the day. A prayer vigil was also held at the bus stop situated in front of the church. On arrival of some members to worship that morning they didn't bother to enter the building but decided to hold hands, encircled the bus stop, and prayed. They were kept posted by my husband, Wendell about my medical condition throughout the day. When the members heard that the first surgery was unsuccessful, the more they prayed.

My illness became a local and global prayer affair. The news of my sudden illness spread like a wild forest fire. Prayer lines became engaged in prayer as soon as they got wind of the situation. As far aas Jamaica, England, Canada, Florida and Texas, you name it, prayer was offered on my behalf. There was a sense of urgency. Pastors and members from other churches, young adults and older members, my in-laws, friends, and acquaintances, attending the same church as I did, all joined in prayer.

Leaders from local conferences and local churches here in the United States also prayed for me. The group comprised members of the Andrews Memorial Seventh-day Adventist Church, Jamaica, West Indies of which my brother-in-law, Vermont and his family are members. Included also in this group who prayed was the Trench Town SDA Church, benevolent committee in the United States, which constitute members from as far as Florida to Pennsylvania, of which I'm a member. They all stormed heaven on my behalf, the minute they heard I was ill.

Children also prayed for me. When I resumed attending midday services on Sabbaths, I can recall a couple sharing with me how they'd hear their little girl, Emily at the time no more than the age of five praying for me each night before going off to sleep. During the period when I was unable to attend church, Every Sabbath Emily made sure to obtain a report from my husband regarding my progress. When I resumed attending midday church service, Emily would take her brother Ethan over to the pew in which I sat and engaged me in a conversation relating to my progress. She always wanted to know how I was doing.

The prayers of the brethren meant so much to me, and I have since learned how effective and powerful united intercessory prayer can be. Every time I think of the power of united intercessory prayer, I'd make reference to the story in Acts 12 in the Bible, regarding the story of Peter who was arrested and thrown into prison, bound in chains, and heavily guarded by soldiers with no chance of escaping. While he was languishing in prison, his brothers and sisters in Christ—the church were holding a united prayer vigil for him. The united prayer meeting was kept at the house of Mary, mother of John

Mark. There the brethren prayed earnestly for Peter's release. Their united, earnest intercessory, prayer bore much fruit. God answered their prayers. He sent an angel to release and guide Peter out of the prison. The narrative states that Peter was fast asleep when the angel struck him on his side and woke him up. The chains on Peter's hands fell off, and the angel instructed him to put on his cloak and sandals and follow him. The angel led Peter past the iron-gate, out in the street and left him. While this mighty miracle was taking place, Peter's brethren were still interceding for him at Mary's house.

Eventually, Peter found his way to Mary's door, where a servant girl by the name of Rhoda answered his knock at the door. She quickly recognized Peter's voice and with excitement went back to tell the others, who were praying, that Peter was at the door. At first they didn't believe that their prayer was already answered and the evidence was now at the doorstep. Peter kept on knocking until they decided to open the door. Peter's miraculous escape from prison was as a result of united, earnest intercessory prayer.

Great and miraculous things do happen when God's people pray. God is still in the prayer-answering business. All we have to do is to call God up and tell Him what we want. I know He will certainly answer in His own time and way. All things are possible but we have to believe and watch God work. The answer we're waiting for is just a prayer away. Ask, believe, and claim. Let's never give up or give in. Even when the situation seems hopeless, let's hold on to faith and *trust* God. He's able. Prayer does change things. Let's never cease from praying. Prayer worked back then for Peter, and it certainly worked for me. It will certainly work for you too. So give it a try today!

"He will be very gracious to you at the sound of your cry; When He hears it, He will answer you" (Isa. 30:19, NKJV).

Global Prayers

By this time the need for prayer became a global affair. The need for God to intervene in my case quickly spread like a California wild forest fire. Prayer had no boundaries. It involved the young and old, male and female. Auntie Maggie and Sis. Arlene along with other members of my parents' and sister's community of faith the Grace Missionary Church back on the island of Jamaica, persevered day and night in prayer on my behalf. Overtime the pastor of this community of faith, Pastor Green along with some members soon became a part of my extended family.

Some of these individuals I've never met, but one day, if we all remain faithful, I'm confident I'll get the chance to meet them. Our meeting might not be in this life but in the life to come at the feet of Jesus. But until then, I'll always have a place in my heart for these dear saints. For the love and support shown through their prayers, cards and many telephone calls.

The news of my illness went as far as to England and Canada. When some of my classmates I attended elementary school, high school, and college with, got wind of my illness, they immediately made contact with my husband. Each one told the other. My husband received several get well cards and telephone calls from many well-wishers, both locally and from across the many bodies of waters. The expression of love and genuine concern regarding my well-being was nonstop and was very much appreciated by my family and me.

On hearing of my sudden illness, my best friend, Joanna from high school days, who presently resides in England, had the brethren of her church, the Gloucester Seventh-day Adventist Church praying for me. She made it her business to get updates every day from my husband regarding my recovery. As she later told me, the members of her church were very anxious to know how

I was progressing. They prayed continually for me, and some still do today. It was a round-the-clock vigil. As a nurse, she knew that most times when an individual suffers a brain aneurysm, it usually resulted in death, so it would have to take a miracle for me to survive and further more beat the odds.

Before immigrating to the United States of America, I attended the Trench Town Seventh-day Adventist Church in Jamaica. I had left this community of believers some years back, and I was overwhelmed when I was told that the members prayed for me on hearing about my illness. At the time I left to live in the United States, some of the present members hadn't yet been born. Some of them were the young adults or children of members I knew and even taught in Sabbath School. Although they didn't know who I was, they had heard my name, but it didn't seem to matter whether they knew me or not; they just became a part of the prayer vigil. I'll always be eternally grateful to these members, both those who knew me and those who didn't, yet they prayed. God heard and answered the local and international cries of the brethren and saw it fit to extend my life.

To God be the glory! On Sunday evening April, 10, 1977, I got baptized at the Trench Town Seventh-day Adventist Church, in Jamaica. Soon, I became friends with a Bible worker who became one of my spiritual mothers in the church. She took me under her wings and nurtured me into the faith until I immigrated to the United States in 1985, putting down roots in the Bronx, New York. All this while we had lost contact with each other, until years after she too immigrated to the United States. We met again one Sabbath at a Trench Town Benevolent service. It was then that I found out that she was living across the border from me.

Each time we saw each other we would spend our time rekindling our relationship by reminiscing about the good old days back there in Trench Town, Jamaica. What does this have to do with my story? On hearing of my illness, she never let up on me. She too joined with the other brethren praying for me. Even after I returned home from rehab, she would call me at least once a week to find out how I was doing. And although her health was failing, she would call to encourage me until she couldn't do it anymore. She's now resting in Jesus, awaiting the first resurrection when we'll see the Blessed Hope (1 Thess. 4:16; Titus 2:13, NKJV).

Another spiritual mother, Sister Mullings, (now deceased), who I met when I became a member of the Trench Town SDA church, also immigrated to the United States and resided in Texas. At the time, on hearing of my illness, this prayer warrior prayed around the clock for me and my other half. She kept in touch with my husband day and night. She called every night from Texas to see if he had gotten home safely after he left work and visited me in the evenings in the rehab. Sis. Mullings also called and prayed with him early in the mornings before he left for work. She really knew what it was to pray without ceasing. (1 Thess. 5:17, KJV). She intentionally had the members of her prayer group praying for us. She knew prayer was the key and could change any bad situation. God was able. Even when she'd go on her vacation and mission trips, she'd still call to find out how things were going.

The reality, I was facing a major crisis in my life. Everything concerning my existence was hanging in the balance. However, I took comfort in the Bible because I had read over and over again many examples of God delivering His people who faced crisis after crisis. And He did so in ways they never had expected. I believe if he did it for them he would certainly do the same for me.

Case in point, I always made a connection with the crisis that arose for the people of God (Esther 3, KJV), when Haman plotted to exterminate them just because Mordecai, Esther's cousin who raised her refused to bow down before him. He became so angry and plotted to kill an entire nation. How could they have escaped death? Mordecai discovered the plot against the Jews and sent messengers to tell Esther about it. Something had to be done. And so the people fasted, and prayed. There was no time to waste. Esther had to take action. She had to see the king as a matter of urgency. Although she was queen, she couldn't present herself unannounced before the king. She had to be called to see him in the inner court. And what was even worse, she knew the Persian law that stated for anyone who presented themself before the king without permission, the consequence would be death.

The only way the person's life could have been spared, was when the king held out his golden scepter. Esther herself was to wait thirty days before she could see the king. But how could she wait for thirty days? There was a crisis. Her people were going to be slaughtered by wicked Haman who, by the way, didn't know that Esther was a Jewess. Esther had to take action after the stern response Mordecai sent her. Finally, she made her decision. She was going in to see the king no matter what. She had made up her mind—do or die. In her final message to Mordecai, she requested that he should gather all the Jews in Shushan, and they should fast and pray. They were to pray day and night about what she was going to do.

Esther, along with her maidens, would become a part of this extended prayer group. The day came when Esther presented herself before King Ahasuerus (Xerxes), and when he saw her sure enough he held out his golden scepter, a sign that he had accepted her unscheduled appearance before him. Her life was spared, while her people were earnestly praying in one accord on her behalf. God answered the fervent prayers of a people who were united in prayer in miraculous ways. A crisis was averted. More prayer more power (Esther 4–5).

"He shall not be afraid of evil tidings: his heart is fixed, trusting in the Lord" (Ps. 112:7, KJV).

Chapter 3

MY FAMILY ARRIVING IN NEW YORK

My parents had to be informed of the news of my illness. They lived on the beautiful island of Jamaica situated in the Caribbean. Who would be the bearer of such sad tidings? Someone had to tell them. Of course that someone was none other than my husband, Wendell. According to my sister, that afternoon the news came first to my brother Lloyd by an international telephone call made by my husband.

My sister Maxine, learned of my illness while she and her husband, along with my parents, were seated in a funeral service. As she told me, she received the sad news calmly in order to share it with our parents. After the funeral service was over, she took our parents to their home, situated one gate away from hers. The first thing she did was to make sure that our parents were seated before she broke the sad news. After she had them comfortably seated, she gently announced in a calm manner that I was hospitalized in a hospital in the Bronx. My parents received the news of my illness in different ways. On hearing the news regarding my hospitalization our mother Iris began to cry, begging God to intervene in the matter. She was overcome by grief and fear. Then suddenly she stopped crying. Why did she stop crying?

I grew up in a Christian home and attended church with my siblings religiously every Sunday morning until my young adult years, when I accepted the Sabbath truth. I grew up with the knowledge that my mom was a praying mother; she prayed daily and trusted God. And she taught her children to pray. As children we were also witnesses to the many times God showed up in our family, such as times when money was needed to pay for exams and other bills. God had never disappointed our family; He was always on time. The money would surely come from somewhere somehow. My mother knew that if she called on the Lord in her distress, He would deliver her. The One who commanded the wind and waves to be still thousands of years ago, was the same One that she prayed to (Ps.107:28–30, KJV). In her heart, she knew that God would work His purpose out. My mother was confident that I was going to pull through whatever I was facing.

I've since asked my mother why she'd stopped crying on hearing that I was hospitalized, and she told me that she was comforted by the fact that the community of faith to which I belonged would take very good care of me. I was in good hands. She knew in her heart that God was in the midst of the situation, whatever it was. She didn't know the extent of my illness until she arrived at the hospital on October 11, 2011. Our father, who was alive at the time, declared in a very superstitious tone "you gone" because he had heard an owl in a tree the night before hooting. My mother has since told me that for a very long period, every night at a certain time, they would hear the sound coming from one of the trees high above the rocks in the backyard. To my father, this was an omen that someone was dying or was going to die, and in my dad's mind, that someone was me.

My sister told me that she'd done her share of crying on hearing the sad news. She had to keep her composure in order to break the news to our parents. She didn't make any further contact with my brother Lloyd who made the initial phone call to her husband regarding the news of my hospitalization. Instead she focused on getting to New York.

My sister shared the news of my illness with her friend Michelle H. who immediately began searching the internet for airline tickets. She managed to secure two tickets that would take my mother and sister to New York. Benedict, my sister's husband, made the decision for them to leave without hesitation. He thought that it was the next sensible and practical thing to do. There was no time to waste. There was a deep sense of urgency. My mother spent the Saturday night packing clothes that would be suitable for the cool weather at that time of year in New York.

So, late Sunday evening on October 10, 2011, my sister and my mother left Jamaica, arriving at the JFK International airport in New York on Monday morning, October 11, 2011. My brother Lloyd accompanied by my father Louis followed, arriving in New York on Thursday, October 13, 2011. When my mother and sister arrived, I was already transferred to the ICU unit.

"For He Himself has said, "I will never leave you nor forsake you" (Heb. 13:5, NKJV).

My Family Arriving in New York

Arriving in New York, my mother and sister were very exhausted from their three-hour-plus flight from Kingston, Jamaica, to the JFK airport. On reaching my home, they both took a cat nap to regain some strength. As soon as they were allowed to visit me in the hospital, they came, accompanied by a dear family friend who we affectionately called "Sis. D". As told to me by these three individuals, the moment they entered the ICU, I recognized who they were and greeted them by their names. However, I addressed my mother as "my mother" and not by my usual term of endearment "mama". Next, I called my sister by her name, Maxine, and then acknowledged the third individual, a dear friend, Sis. D. That Monday was relatively quiet for me as I recuperated in the ICU. Then Tuesday came, and both my mother and sister came back to see me some time during the day.

In the meantime, my husband Wendell had to work. The bills had to be paid. My mother Iris and sister Maxine told me that the Tuesday following was a difficult one. They thought the icy hand of death had finally arrived to snatch me. My life hung in the balance. I became restless. The doctors on my case told my husband, mother, and sister that I was facing another challenge.

They were told that I'd developed pneumonia and was having difficulty breathing on my own. Something had to be quickly done. So the decision was made to make an opening in my throat and insert a tracheal tube from the larynx to the bronchi, which would transport air to and from my lungs and windpipe to assist me with my breathing. This new development called for more prayer. Divine intervention was still needed. However, the plan to slit my throat and insert a trachea was short lived. By divine intervention the plan was aborted. There was no need for a trachea anymore. I began breathing on my own. My God came through once again. He's never too late, He's never too early, but always on time. He's really an on-time God. Prayer was still being said on my behalf. My case was carried into the throne room where the prayers of the saints were offered by Jesus to the Father on my behalf.

My mother had a difficult time staying in the ICU, so she left and went outside in the hallway. My sister had to persuade her to return to the ICU, which she eventually did. A doctor, who happened to be in the ICU at the time, made the suggestion to my mother to speak continuously with me. According to my mother, the doctor told her that although my eyes were closed and I wasn't able to speak with her, I was still able to hear. The doctors had previously told my husband that the next forty-eight hours were critical ones, but God was on the case. He was hearing the humble cry of all the people praying on my behalf locally and globally. The days I spent in ICU consisted of touch-and-go moments. On some days, it seemed as if the grim reaper—death—was lurking in shadows to snatch me away from my loved ones, while other days were calm, peaceful, and hopeful. God was not finished with me yet. He was going to finish what He'd started (Phil. 1:6, KJV).

"Angels came and ministered unto Him"
(Matt. 4:11, KJV).

A Visit from an Angel and a Cryptic Message

I finally made it through the forty-eight critical hours, and on Friday, October 21, 2011, I was transferred from the critical care unit to a hospital room. The hospital room was located right in front of the nurse's station on the third floor. I still was in need of critical care that called for twenty-four hours of round-the-clock supervision from both doctors and nurses alike. As the days turned into nights and nights turned into days, my medical prognosis improved. I was now able to receive visits from other members of my family, church family, and friends and acquaintances. During this time, I was still connected to huge medical equipment, with tubes and cords that connected me to the machines. I was told that the hair at the back of my head was fully shaven, along with the section over my right eye. For a while, for reasons unknown, I'd stopped talking. However, in a few days I was talking again. I've since been told that my eyes were constantly closed but every now and then I would open them. However, I recognized persons who visited by the sound of their voices. I cannot remember doing this.

To this day I can't recall or remember what really happened, who visited, who called, or who said what. Members of my family were the ones who told to me about friends, who visited me in the hospital. So, on my post-op visit to see my neurologist, my first question to him was, why wasn't I able to recall all that had transpired during my hospitalization.

He explained to me why I was unable to remember what had occurred. This was due to the fact that my brain had gone through a very traumatic event. It was as if it had literally put up a 'door' and slammed it shut, never to be reopened again. This was how the brain had chosen to protect itself. Since then, I'm only able to remember where I was when I fell ill, the trip on the ambulance to rehab, the time spent in rehab, and my many therapy sessions. To this day, I'm still unable to recall what transpired during my hospital stay. I had to and still do rely on what has been told to me regarding my time in ICU.

Did I believe in angels? Yes I did! And even today I still do. I've read in the Bible that angels were ministering spirits (Heb. 1:14, KJV) along with many stories of individuals having encounters with them, such as Abraham, Jacob, Elijah, Daniel, and Peter, and the list goes on and on.

Angels were used by God to announce the mega news of Jesus' birth. They were used by God to deliver His people when they faced crises, challenges, and persecution from their enemies. It is my strong belief that angels are still active in the lives of God's children today, especially those who are in the mission field, proclaiming the gospel of Jesus Christ, facing death, hardship, and persecution because of their faith.

My sister, affectionately called Miss Max, related an incident that happened one day when she visited me in the hospital. She said she was sitting in a chair next to my bed, when she noticed I had a huge smile on my face. She said I pointed to the door and asked her: "Do you see the angel?" She replied, "No!" She couldn't see the angel I was telling her about. I then proceeded to give her a detailed description of what the angel looked like, how the angel was dressed, and what the angel did while in the room.

On entering the hospital room, the angel made her way to the huge medical equipment situated next to my bed. According to my sister, I described her as having dark complexion. She told me that I used my eyes to follow the unseen guest and gave her a detailed description of what was happening. There were tubes that connected me to the machines, and the unseen visitor took her time and meticulously checked each one. I guess she was checking to see if the machines were functioning properly and the tubes were in the right places.

After completing her thorough check of each tube, the angel proceeded to walk around my bed, seeing to it that I was comfortable. She went from the top of the bed and then made her way to the foot of the bed. According to the expression on her face, she seemed to have been satisfied with what she had seen. Finally, after making her thorough checks, she turned and made her way exiting through the door. I told my sister that the individual I had described to her was my angel. My sister told me that throughout the angel's visit, my face was aglow and remained that way even after the angel left the room. To this day, I've been unable to recall the encounter I had with my guardian angel.

While I was recuperating in a rehabilitation facility, I had a second encounter with the same angel. My bed was situated next to a huge glass window, and at nights, the light from the pole on the street would pierce through the window pane and shone directly on the curtain at the bottom of my bed. One night, as I laid in between the sheets, I needed help to go to the washroom. There was no one around to assist me. All was quiet in the facility. The other patient in the room was fast asleep. The buzzer on my bed wasn't working, so I couldn't call the nurse's station for help. So, I laid quietly in the dark, thinking how I was going to reach the restroom. When suddenly I saw a hand grasping the curtain on which the light from the street was shining. The hand was of a dark complexion.

Next, I saw a head, with short, black, natural hair. It was a lady. She had a smile on her face. From her pear-shaped eyes, she looked at me and said, "Would you care to use the restroom?" I quickly answered, "Yes." The woman quietly opened up the curtain hanging from the pole and moved the wheelchair behind it closer to my bed. Because I was unable to walk, she slowly helped me into the wheelchair and quietly wheeled me past the bed of the other patient who was still fast asleep.

She opened the door of the restroom situated at the entrance of the room, and with her assistance, I was able to use it. After, I'd finished using the rest room, she wheeled me back to my bed, helped me back in bed, and put the curtain back in the position where she'd found it. I told her thanks, and she left. From that night onward and days that followed, especially when I went for physical therapy sessions, I'd look out for the lady who helped me that night but never saw her. I'm convinced that the same lady "angel" who visited me that day in the hospital and I'd described to my sister was the same lady who assisted me that night in the rehabilitation facility.

"But they could not read the writing, nor make known to the king the interpretation thereof" (Dan. 5:8, KJV).

My Family Arriving in New York

Two adult members of my community of faith, as I was told visited me religiously every day. I've no memory of this ever happening. But with eyes wide opened and a big grin on my face, I'd called them by their names and asked them to move closer to my bedside. I'd engaged them in many conversations, but to this day, I have no clue of this ever taking place. For some reason or another, or so I was told, I'd used a clipboard with a piece of paper attached to it, along with a pen as my means of communicating with others. Whenever I wanted to communicate, I'd scribbled on pieces of paper. It became difficult to decipher what I'd to say. What I wrote made no sense to the person reading it, and sometimes it would take more than one individual to decipher the message I was trying to convey. This was my hieroglyphics!

After hearing what had transpired back then in the hospital room, the book of Daniel, chapter 5 to be exact, came to my mind. In this chapter of Daniel, there was a king by the name of Belshazzar who had a great feast, and he invited many guests. He drank wine with those in attendance from the sacred goblets his grand-father Nebuchadnezzar had taken from the temple in Jerusalem when he took the children of Israel into captivity into Babylon.

As they drank from the sacred vessels, the fingers of a hand appeared and began writing on the wall. The king enquired of his soothsayers, astrologers, and magicians to interpret the writing and they couldn't. Then he heard about Daniel who was able to interpret the writing on the wall. I was no king, neither was I having a party, nor was I drinking wine from sacred vessels. I was very ill, and I needed to have my hieroglyphics interpreted. I had no need of soothsayers, astrologers, or magicians; I just needed someone to interpret what I'd written. I just needed a modern-day Daniel, and I ended up having more than three to decipher what I'd written. What was I trying to say? According to my sister, she along with the other two "Daniels", Elder Icene, and her daughter, Dr. Kadine, were able to decipher my hieroglyphics, although it took them a long time to figure it out.

They finally got it! I was making a request. I was asking Dr. Kadine, a member of the church I attended for assistance. She happened to be a Christian, a quiet, unassuming professional adult. She was a trained, licensed physical therapist. Don't ask me how I knew that I was going to need physical therapy; your guess is as good as mine because I don't have an answer for you. This was what the three interpreters figured out from what I'd written. I guess all this and more will be revealed to me when I see my Maker and King face to face. I just accepted and went along with what was told to me.

In a chapter to follow, you'll read about how God used Dr. Kadine to help me at a time when I desperately needed additional physical therapy.

"I will instruct thee and teach thee in the way which thou shalt go: I will guide thee with mine eye" (Ps. 32:8, KJV).

Chapter 4

Choosing a Rehab Facility and Transferred

All this time while I was recuperating, my other half was busy trying to find a suitable rehabilitation program for me to enter after my discharge from the hospital. I still wasn't in a position to go home. I still needed more care.

My case was classified as acute rehabilitation. So he collaborated with the social worker assigned to my case at the hospital and I was transferred to a facility which was regarded as one of the best in New York City. Yes, this facility was renowned for its track record in the area of stroke rehabilitation.

The program I entered was very intensive. My husband saw to it that I got the best quality care offered around town. But there was one problem. Accessibility. He has since told me that yes, he wanted the best service for me but he had to take other factors into consideration to make the final decision. The first choice was the ideal but it was situated too far from where we lived.

Secondly, the commute to and from home would not have been convenient for him, especially with regards to distance and time. Thirdly, my parents, and other members of my family along with our friends would not have had easy access to transportation if and when they wanted to visit. Finally, along with much prayer, seeking God's direction, and with the continued help from the social worker at the hospital, a decision was made.

The main reason why this rehab facility was chosen was because of its accessibility. It could be reached by the New York City subway system from any direction, car or bus, no matter what time of day or night it was. The arrangements for my transfer to rehab were eventually finalized. And after spending approximately seventeen days at a hospital in the Northern section of the Bronx, I was discharged on Tuesday, October 25, 2011 and transported by an ambulance, to my new 'home' rehab.

"Behold I am with you and will keep you wherever you go…" (Gen. 28:15, NKJV).

The Road to Recovery Begins in Rehab

I was accompanied to the rehab center by my sister because my other half had to work. I was strapped to a stretcher and pushed in the ambulance. As I laid on the stretcher with my eyes closed, I could still hear the doors of the ambulance opened and slammed shut. Next to follow was the start of the engine, then I was in full motion. I never had a clue as to where I was heading.

Life had to go on. I knew my sister was with me because I could hear her having a conversation with someone. I'd no clue who the next person was, until it was revealed to me many days later by my sister who the individual was. My eyes remained closed the entire time of the journey and I was just depending on my sense of hearing to know what was going on at the time.

The ride was very bumpy. As we went along, I could tell when we hit potholes. At one point I got the sense that we were stuck in traffic for a long time because we didn't move for a while and the ride was taking longer than expected. After some time we finally reached our destination.

The next sound I heard were doors opening up. Then the stretcher I was strapped on was lifted out of the ambulance. Doors were slammed shut again. I could hear more voices this time and it seemed as if my sister was giving personal information to the individuals she was talking with. After some time had passed, I was taken to a room which some days later I found out was situated across from the nurse's station. I figured that if I was placed in a room across from the nurse's station, then my illness was very grave.

On the night I settled in my new place of abode, I heard a faint voice calling my name. I opened my eyes and I saw a stately figure standing at my bedside. I was able to make out that the individual was a female. She was dressed in white, and presented as a motherly figure. She introduced herself by name and told me that she was my nurse for the night. I can't remember giving her a verbal response but I believe I just closed my eyes again and went to sleep. From the way she spoke it would seemed that she was gentle and kind.

When morning came, and I forced my eyes opened and tried keeping them open, the stately figure dressed in white that I'd seen the night before was nowhere around. It seemed she'd vanished into thin air. Then I recalled that she'd told me that she was my nurse for the night. So I guess her shift was over and she'd left for home.

It was now Wednesday, October 26, 2011. At around seven-thirty, a nurse's assistant came to my bedside. My bed was turned into a make-shift bathroom, and I was given a sponge bath. I would be the recipient of many more sponge baths on weekends. From Mondays to Fridays between the hours of five o'clock and five-thirty in the mornings, I would receive showers. In the mornings, the nurse's attendant would help me prepare for my showers.

On the third day in my new "home," and after receiving my sponge bath and breakfast, I had visits from three individuals. The first one told me that she was going to be my speech therapist. Shortly after, another came by and informed me that she was going to be my occupational therapist. Finally, the last individual who came by to see me was a physical therapist. Why did I need these people? Speech therapy for what? Occupational therapy for what? As to physical therapy, why? Why did I need all these services? The visit from the three therapists didn't reveal much information but a description of what the days ahead would be like. After the therapists concluded their visits, I finally closed my eyes and went to sleep. It was a good feeling. That's all I wanted to do. However, I spent many days getting acquainted with my new surroundings, taking in the varied sights and sounds.

On weekdays, a flurry of activities would take place on the side of the hospital floor I was on. Early in the mornings, the attendant would take her precious cargo in a wheelchair, down the corridor to the shower stall. As we traveled along, we would see other attendants hurrying to get to the rooms of other patients. On reaching the shower room, the attendant would push my wheelchair in the shower stall. After removing the gown I had on, she soaped me and the next thing I felt was water cascading from my head, over the wheelchair, and reaching to the ground where a hole was for the water to escape. Next, I was dried off with a towel and had a change of clothing.

The attendant would always go in the opposite direction, when she was taking me back to my room, to avoid bumping into other patients who were on their way to the shower stall. On reaching my room, the attendant would assist me in getting into bed and get me dressed for my scheduled therapy sessions for the day. The times for showering and eating became a routine, but not so with the therapy sessions. There were days when the times had to be changed because of other activities. I didn't look forward to those early morning showers. I couldn't bear the idea of getting up so early in the mornings to take a shower. I would often asked myself the questions: Why couldn't she have found another patient who was willing to take an early morning shower? Why me? However, I didn't rebel, and I didn't want to put on display any selfish behaviors. There were other patients who were in need of a sponge bath or a shower, and there were far too many. So I counted my blessing and felt a sense of gratitude that I was among the first set of patients to get a shower early in the mornings.

Automatically, turning to lay on my sides proved impossible for me to do. After sleeping for many years on my left side, it now became a thing of the past. I had to get accustomed to lying on my back day in day out, whether I was awake or asleep. This continued for approximately two years until one day, I found myself automatically lying on my left side again. That was excitement for me. From then on I returned to my normal sleeping style. What a relief that was for me. I'd jumped a challenging hurdle.

As time went by it was still a difficult task for me to keep my eyes opened. The nurses who were positioned at the station made every effort to see that I did just that. To accomplish this they kept calling me several times by my first name. Looking back it was their way of preventing me from slipping into a state of unconsciousness.

Double vision became a part of my torment. Opposite my bed was a dry erase board situated next to a clock on the wall with my therapy schedule for the day. Situated next to a clock on the wall. I would see two dry erase boards, two clocks, two lights, and two nurses when there was only one. I passed my days seeing doubles. There were times when I would close my right eye and open the left eye, or blink both eyes to see if I could get rid of the doubles, but it was not that easy. The doubles wouldn't go away. They persisted!

The physical therapist would hold up before my face a popsicle stick with a large green circle on it. The green circle was my focal point. Then she would ask me to follow the green circle as she moved her right hand from left to right. As the days went by, I gradually began to see less and less of the doubles and was able to keep my eyes opened for longer periods of time.

Every morning at eleven o'clock, the first person that saw me was the physical therapist. As she approached my bed, I noticed she always had a wheelchair with her. She positioned the wheelchair in close proximity to my bed. Then, in a soft voice she asked, "Can you move to the edge of the bed please?" I would slowly shuffle my torso to the edge of the bed and then she assisted me into the wheelchair. It was during my first physical therapy session that I realized that I was unable to walk. Here, I saw two feet attached to my body, and I was unable to move them on my own.

My feet were lifeless. Because of this I knew that something was radically wrong. My world began to turn upside down. Something was wrong with my feet. Was I seeing right? Something had gone wrong! What was it? I needed answers. Who would be willing to give me the answers I needed? No one had told me why I couldn't walk. I guess they were all afraid to break the news to me. I had to find this out for myself.

During weekdays, I was wheeled through the door of the room I was sharing with another patient by the physical therapist. After making the right turn at the nurse's station, she hurriedly pushed the wheelchair down the long corridor. With no exchange of words, the therapist continued pushing the wheelchair with its cargo. All my senses kicked into high gear. On the left side of the corridor I could see other wheelchairs in different sizes and shapes, lined up in a neat row next to the wall. Some of the people moving around were dressed in white, green, blue, and red outfits.

I assumed that some were doctors, nurses, and attendants. They were attending to other individuals who seemed to be patients lying on beds or seated in wheelchairs like myself. On the right side of the corridor were unoccupied beds, and I could hear voices, moans, and groans coming from behind curtains drawn. I knew I was on my way to "somewhere." But where was that somewhere? I continued to take in the different sights and sounds as we traveled along.

All this time, I was unaware that I had lost the hearing in my right ear. I was still puzzled and kept wondering in silence as to the reason why I was in such a place. Then the wheelchair came to a sudden stop, and a huge wooden door opened up before me. Next, the therapist wheeled me into the room. On entering the room, the first thing I did was to look around.

I noticed that the room was very large, and from all appearances, it looked like a place where people did exercises. The equipment in the room varied in shapes and sizes, and there were several individuals in it. The folks were either talking or were engaged in what appeared to be exercises. The physical therapist took me over to a corner of the room and told me that we'd be working together for one hour every day. I'd be doing exercises for balancing and coordination. She began with some strength exercises, and as time went on, I gradually found out that I had a brain aneurysm that had left me unable to walk, balance, and coordinate movement.

By this time, I was now able to keep my eyes opened for longer periods without a nurse coercing me to do so. I was now fully acquainted with my new surroundings but just couldn't adjust because it was still not home to me. I missed being in my personal space, and yearned for the day to come when I would go back home.

On entering the room that was my temporary 'home', the bathroom was situated on the left, and there were shelves and cupboards on either side for us patients to keep our personal belongings. Next to each bed was a chair for anyone who visited to sit. From my bed I could see a flurry of activities, at the nurse's station situated in front of the door. My bed was next to a huge picture window. From there, early in the mornings I would witness the sun casting its rays of yellows and oranges on its horizon. Then gradually shining in its brilliance on the towering skyscrapers and the miniature buildings in the foreground on the other side.

In the evenings, the sun would descend showing off its orange-and-brown hues as if it were saying, "I'm going off to sleep now; I'll see you at dawn, so until then, goodbye. There were days when the sky presented itself as a picture of gray, a symbol of disappointment, despair, and depression. It was even worse whenever it rained. I just wanted out. There were days when I wanted to go home so badly;

I felt trapped by my circumstances, and feeling down. I had to find an escape route.

"And David was greatly distressed...but David encouraged himself in the Lord his God" (I Sam. 30:6, KJV).

There was a time when I went as far as hatching an escape plan with a friend, who at the time lived in Brooklyn. She came to visit one day, and I just took the opportunity to lay out my escape route to her. While in rehab, my brother Mark, Margaret and Verne were my constant visitors. Although I was going through a roller coaster of emotions, I didn't have trouble sleeping at nights. I slept like a baby right through the nights. Emotionally, some days were better than others. However, there were still many questions to be answered. Because I was still in the dark, remaining clueless.

Getting up and sitting in a wheelchair wasn't an easy task for me. Each time I had to get-up or sit-up I had to be assisted by an attendant. I couldn't do anything on my own. I realized I'd to rely on the Sovereign God who knew the end from the beginning. I was convinced that with God on my side I would be able to do anything if I relied on Him for strength (Phil. 4:13, KJV).

Each day, I was given a menu sheet from which to choose the foods I wanted eat for breakfast, lunch, and dinner. Every day I religiously had the same foods to eat. For breakfast, which lasted from eight-thirty to nine o'clock, I'd have a ripe banana or an orange, a bowl of hot oatmeal, and a corn muffin.

Lunch time was usually from twelve-thirty to one o'clock. I ate cooked vegetables and creamed potato with baked chicken. Dinner time was usually around six o'clock, and I would have the same foods for dinner. For desert, I would have some ice-cream or jello. I never cared much for supper. My food choices remained the same until I was discharged from the rehab facility.

I gradually was able to sit up with two huge pillows propped up behind my back. It was still difficult to turn and lay on either sides. I was constantly on my back with my head rested on two white pillows, with both eyes closed. Although there was another patient in the room, it seemed as if I was alone. Sometimes my mind became like a blank slate and would remain that way for very long periods of time. And there were times when I found myself praying.

Being unable to move also impacted my personal hygiene, due to the fact that I wasn't able to take care of myself. I needed daily assistance even to leave the hospital bed to use the bathroom. I thought this was not going to be a big deal. But it was! I thought in no time I would be well again and return to my passion, teaching. But as the days went by, I gradually found that I was very ill and that I wouldn't be returning to teaching any time soon. This wasn't going to be a walk over. A huge feat was ahead of me. I realized that I had to learn to walk all over again. I felt like a baby.

It seemed as if I'd never walked before. What would I do? What would be next? The days I spent in rehab went something like this: I got up before five o'clock every weekday morning, took an early bath, got groomed, ate breakfast, one hour of physical therapy, one hour of occupational therapy, and one hour of speech therapy, lunch, and spending the evening hours in bed.

Sometimes, I would have two different speech providers, and the speech sessions would consist of the four basic number operations (addition, subtraction, multiplication, and division), presented in mental and math word problem, working with money and telling time. Reading newspaper articles, and identifying the main idea and working on analogies. There were instances when I would also be engaged in speech therapy group sessions. The group therapy sessions were once per week and consisted of a retired librarian, a social worker, and me and the in-house speech therapist as the facilitator. I was soon to realize that some of the strategies I'd used with my special needs students as a special education teacher would help me in my recovery. So, I began using them especially to help me with my speech issues.

I resented going to physical and occupational therapy sessions because I just didn't want to leave my bed—my comfort zone. It was the best place for me to be. I was contented doing speech therapy sessions when the provider came to me in my bed. I didn't want to do any form of physical exercise. The occupational therapist would take me to an assimilated car, bathroom, and kitchen on the floor below the one that became my "home" for two weeks and six days. There, she would teach me how to enter and exit a car, use a kitchen and a bathroom, as if I'd never done those things before. It felt very, very strange and awkward. Why did I have to do all of that stuff?

Soon I realized that it was important and necessary for me to be re-taught those kind of activities. I was receiving services that would help me get back to my normal way of living, after experiencing a brain aneurysm that could have taken my life. There were daily living skills that I'd completely forgotten how to do independently, so I guess that's why it was called *rehabilitation*. It was more than I'd thought.

The road to recovery was not going to be a piece of cake or a walk over. I realized it was going to be a huge hurdle for me. Little did I know what was awaiting ahead of me. My *life* would never be the same! Each day after my therapy sessions were over, I would go back to bed, and with both eyes closed, prayed and sought encouragement in the Lord my God. Although a television was directly before me on the wall, I had no interest in watching it.

Like David, I found myself doing just what he did in (1 Sam. 30:6, KJV). After being pursued by King Saul, David decided to take up residence in Philistine country. There he formed friendship with King Achish, a king of the Philistines. The king gave David the town of Ziglag to live in. So David and his 600 men and their families took up residence in Ziglag. There was a time when David was away from Ziglag, making plans with the Philistines to fight his people Israel. However, the Philistines didn't trust David per adventure in the middle of the battle he would turn against them. So, King Ashish had no choice but to part ways with David. David returned to Ziglag only to find that the city was burned to the ground by the Amalekites, cattle, wives and children were all gone. Desolation was as far as his eyes could see.

Even David's two wives, Ahinoam of Jezreel and Abigail the widow of Carmel, were also taken and everything destroyed, David's men became angry and turned against him and blamed him for the destruction, (1 Sam. 30:6, KJV). What was David to do? Where could David seek solace? His men were about to take his life. David was overcome with despair, discouragement, and depression. He was caught between a rock and a hard place! However, David found strength in the Lord. "Why art thou cast down, O my soul, and why art thou disquieted in me? Hope thou in God; for I shall yet praise him for the help of his countenance (Ps. 42:5, KJV).

Like David I too experienced the 3Ds. I could relate to David. I felt as if someone had stripped me of my career, livelihood and years of service. The future looked very bleak. I was at a dark place in my life. Everywhere I turned, it was if a door slammed shut with no sign of reopening. It seemed like nothing was going my way. Where was the best place for me to go? I decided to look to the scriptures to help me with my faith. For a while my emotions ran high. But with prayer, constantly reading the scriptures and listening to spiritual songs, I managed by God's love, mercy, and grace to hold on and never let go.

But for the mercies of God I never went over the precipice of depression. It was only a thin line between madness and sanity. I was aware that once I went over the line there would be no turning back. I'd end up spending the rest of my life popping pills. During this dark period of my life I knew of a certain God kept me! And His promises never failed! I'd spent many days reading Bible stories about Jesus: how He loved people, how he healed people, and how He showed compassion as He mingled with them. He was the Healer!

All it took was for the individuals around Jesus to believe and reach out in faith. I knew that Jesus loved me also. I never doubted His love for me, like the woman who touched the hem of his garment and exercised her faith and was healed, (Luke 8:43-48 KJV), I too could have a similar experience. There were also times, like a broken record, the song "It took a Miracle of Love and Grace" kept playing over and over in my head. I didn't know what the future had in store for me. There was so many uncertainties.

God was so good to me! My husband Wendell, came to see me every day, whether it rained or shined, evening, and morning, early or late. He collected my soiled clothes, took them home, washed them, and brought them back either the next morning on his way to work or in the evenings on his way back home. He made sure I had the correct clothing and shoes for my physical therapy sessions. Some mornings on his way to work, he would take a ripe banana when he stopped by and would go as far as to meet the dietician to make sure that I was getting my dietary requirements met.

Wendell has since told me that I became very happy when he would come to see me on his way home from work. And as soon as it was time for him to leave, I became very sad. He was my rock. Wendell made sure I was well taken care of and I had everything I needed. He took very good care of me and still do. I never lacked anything. I felt his love and devotion at all times.

It was my privilege to have both my parents visiting me almost every evening. And Wendell was the one who made it happened. My sister Maxine, showed both my elderly parents how to navigate the subway system to and fro to visit me at the rehab facility in the city, before returning home to the island of Jamaica. Every evening my father took the lead protecting my mother on the subway until

I returned permanently home. While in the rehab, I was also visited by family members, my prayer partner and members of my community of faith.

Slowly, the days dragged on. However, I was determined to leave rehab the Wednesday before Thanksgiving Day, Thursday, November 24, 2011. I had made a pledge to myself that by God's grace I would get out of there, and get out I did. I wanted to be where I was familiar with my own space. And sure enough, I was discharged exactly the day before Thanksgiving. I was really tired of getting up early in the mornings, and being one of the first patient to be wheeled to the shower, eating the same breakfast, lunch, and dinner day after day, not to mention therapy until bedtime, when the lights were turned off.

There were times while in rehab that I would often have flashbacks of teaching and would create pictures in my head of giving support to children with learning disabilities. At the time when I became ill, I was a licensed, practicing, special education teacher, teaching at a public school in the City. I enjoyed working with the students at the school where I taught. My passion was to teach children how to become functionally literate and independent. At this particular school, I was the special education teacher support services provider, charged with the responsibility to educate children classified with mild, moderate, or severe learning disabilities and those that made up the at-risk population and needed early intervention.

The disabilities ranged from dyslexia, dysgraphia, dyscalculia, speech, disorganization, interpersonal relationship skills, autism, the emotionally disturbed, and more. As I taught my students from day to day, I found out that they all learned differently. One size didn't fit all. I had to align my instructions with the school curriculum, keeping in mind the individualized goals on each student's Individualized Educational Plan (IEP). It was also my responsibility to assess and implement differentiated instructions to assist my learning disability students. When planning lessons, I also had to take into account each student's learning styles, (visual, auditory, kinesthetic, tactile), grouping them according to their abilities (strengths and weaknesses), interests, engaging in formal and informal assessments on a continuous basis, and tweaking lessons to meet the varied needs when necessary—all *strategies*!

Meeting with classroom teachers on grade levels and service providers was a must. It was a team effort to educate these children. In conjunction with my teaching responsibility, I was also the liaison for all matters related to special education in the school, whether internally or externally. Externally, I'd attend all professional development workshops and turn-keyed the information to the administrative staff, teaching staff, and service providers at the school. I was the go-to person for all inquiries related to all IEPs, belonging to the special education population ranging from kindergarten to grade five in the school.

It was also my responsibility to oversee that students were receiving all their mandated services—speech, occupational therapy, physical therapy, and counseling, and that the school was in compliance with the Department of Education protocols as it relates to IEPs that were written on time, whether it was yearly or triennial reviews. I also oversaw the scheduling of all (IEP) meetings with teachers, parents, guardians, and all service providers. In the absence of the principal, I would serve as the District Representative on the Pupil Personnel Team (PPT) at meetings.

As the district representative on the team, I was privileged to work with the guidance counselor, the school psychologist, the social worker, the speech and language therapists, and the physical and occupational therapists. As a team, it was our job to identify, discuss, and make recommendations for students referred for special education services, and others who did not have an IEP but were considered at-risk students.

All I wanted to do, was to get back to the task of teaching. I loved what I did. It was gratifying to me when the students I taught eventually learned a skill and was able to make the application without my help. In the days that followed, I realized that it was just a dream. It would never to be. My days of teaching were behind me. I always thought that God had given me the gift of teaching, as I had been told many times by my mother and other acquaintances, even people I'd met for the first time in my life.

I had never submitted an application for the teaching position I had at the time. I can recall quite clearly one Sunday night in November 1998, while sitting at my dining room table working on an assignment (I was pursuing my master's degree in teaching at the time), when I received a telephone call that would lead me to my dream teaching position. I knew I was speaking to a female on the other side of the telephone. As the conversation continued, I tried to identify the voice but couldn't. The next thing I heard in my ears was, "Are you interested in a teaching position?" I sheepishly replied yes, without asking what teaching position she was offering me. Next, I heard, "You can attend an interview at any time convenient to you."

At the time, I was permanently employed at another city agency, so I was in no rush in moving to another place of employment. However, the offer sounded too good to be true. I just couldn't pass the offer up. I didn't go looking for the job; the job came to me. I then asked her, "Can I attend an interview tomorrow?" The next day was a Monday. The reply came back "Sure!" I scheduled an interview with her for 4:30 p.m. the next evening. She gave me the address of the school and even the train that would get me there. And that's history.

So how could the God I served, allowed all I'd achieved to go up in smoke? I went to school part time, holding down a full-time job, running to board the train every evening, running and walking to get to classes after getting off work at 3:30 p.m. in order to be on time at 4:00 p.m. I couldn't be late. Being late was a no, no.

I did this for seven and a half years on Tuesdays, Wednesdays, and even on Thursdays. I had to endure many train delays and detours at all hours of the night, getting home sometimes at midnight, and waking up very early in the mornings to get to work. I forfeited even my summer holidays. I had worked very hard, paid my dues, and then this!

"I tell you, take your mat and go home" (Mark 2:11, NIV).

Chapter 5

HOME SWEET HOME

I really didn't care what the outcome was going to be like. My mind was made up. I wanted to go home, and home I was determined to go. I didn't care about leaving rehab on a mat, or walking out (if I could), or being wheeled out. Whichever way it went, I wanted out of there!

My rehab admission date was Tuesday, October 25, 2011, and my exit interview was Tuesday, November 22, 2011. As I was wheeled into the conference room to the exit interview, I saw seated around a large, what seemed to be an oak, oval-shaped table, my husband Wendell, the social worker responsible for my case, and the physical and occupational therapists. Missing from my exit interview was the lead speech provider. However, her report regarding my case was presented by one of the other therapists present. I was finally granted my release.

The next day at mid-morning my husband along with a dear friend Alberto, came and got me from the rehab. I said my goodbyes to the friends I had made: nurses, nursing attendants, and patients alike. Then my husband wheeled me on to the elevator, and on reaching the lobby, I was taken to the car that would take me home. It was a crisp fall morning. I could feel the coolness of the morning as I was lifted from the wheelchair and gently placed in the back seat of the car. With all doors closed, the engine started. We were finally on our way home.

As I traveled along, I felt like I'd gained my freedom after being locked away that seemed a very long time. It felt so good to be on the outside again. Just to breathe God's fresh air, and to feel the rays of the sun on my cheeks, on a crisp fall day was such a liberating feeling. I felt really free! As we drove along, I noticed that some trees had lost their leaves and had gone off to sleep, while others showed off their beautiful foliage; the yellows, the oranges, and browns.

The words *"love and grace!"* from a famous song kept going over and over in my head. Yes, I realized that I should have died *but* God! I felt as if I was given a second chance to live. It was my responsibility to make good use of this second chance. It was then that I purposed in my heart that I would never ask God to give me the reason why He allowed me to get ill. I knew that although I couldn't make sense of what was happening, this was a chance to build my trust in Sovereign God. It was a difficult thing for me to do, but I had to risk it all on this God I'd been serving over thirty-something years.

I didn't leave the rehab facility on a mat. Instead I left in a wheelchair and a car; but there was a huge problem that gave much cause for concern awaiting me at home. My bedroom was on the second floor of the house I lived in. How was I going to get up those stairs? On returning home, with his strong arms, my father lifted me out of the car and swiftly carried me up the stairs to my bedroom. I never went back to the first floor unless I had a doctor's appointment. God, the great Problem Solver, took care of the problem.

Night eventually came, and what a good feeling it was to be in mine own bed approximately five-plus weeks. As I laid in bed, it was as if I heard someone saying to me "I AM THAT I AM. Whatever you want Me to, be I'll be." I looked over to the nightstand next to me, and I saw my Bible. I kept on grasping for it until it was finally in my hand.

I knew of a story in the Old Testament in the book of Exodus, that had some connection with the statement I heard in my head. So, I turned to the book of Exodus and began reading from chapter one. I finally found the statement in chapter three. There, I read where God wanted Moses to go down to Egypt and tell the children of Israel that the God of their fathers was going to deliver them out of captivity. Moses then asked God, if Pharaoh should ask for the name of the person who sent him what answer should he give. God's reply to Moses was; "I AM WHO I AM (Exod. 3:14, NKJV). I wondered what this statement had to do with me.

The weeks went into months, and months into years, I gradually saw how the statement slowly became meaningful in my life. I internalized it as, "Whatever you want Me to be to you, I'll be!" Jesus became the Source of my strength. He became my Provider, my Comforter, my Deliverer, and my Healer. I realized that it was Jesus and me on the journey of faith. I had to trust Him and took Him at His Word. It was total dependency!

In the days leading up to my home going from rehab, my father Louis (now deceased) was the one who received and assembled all the assistive devices that I would be needing to be mobile. Apart from a wheelchair I was going to use a walker and a bath chair. He also took on the task of using a roll of silver duct tape to firmly secure the rugs on the floor to prevent me from tripping. So, when I got home, these safety measures were already in place. Later on, as I began to walk, he used yellow masking tape to denote the edges of the steps on the staircase.

More accommodations and modifications had to be put in place, especially for my safety. One day, my father and my dear friend Joanna, a nurse, who came from England to assist in taking care of me went to a department store and purchased a hand-held shower for me. The shower was the latest addition to the bathroom. I still had difficulty sitting up in bed and on the bath chair.

With assistance, I had to take showers sitting on the bath chair with the hand held shower in my hand. Because of the circumstance in which I now found myself, I truly understood the importance of assistive devices, special accommodations and modifications. As a special education teacher, these words were part of my vocabulary. I used them in my practice every day as I made recommendations for the special needs students I taught. What was theory had now become practical for me.

On my first few visits to see the neurosurgeon and a neuro-radiologist, it was my father and mother and a neighbor (now deceased), who took me to the appointments. My husband had to work. The bills had to be paid. This went on for approximately a month after leaving rehab. By this time, Joanna had returned to England. She came, she prayed, she did, she kept in touch, and she encouraged. Feeding and dressing myself was a challenge. I had to depend on my husband and mother to take care of me, my mother Iris was my caregiver in the days and my husband Wendell was my caregiver at nights.

By now, my father had returned to Jamaica because he was being treated for prostate cancer. He and my mother had agreed that she'd stay behind and continue to assist my Wendell to take care of me. It was then that my nephews, Maxine two sons, Geordan and Nicholas, came and spent the Christmas holidays with me.

"You will keep him in perfect peace, Whose mind is stayed on You; because he trusts in You" (Isa. 26:3 NKJV).

Chapter 6

ROAD TO RECOVERY CONTINUES AT HOME

Now at home, I was assigned Visiting Nursing Service (VNS). This service was arranged by my social worker before I left the rehab center. The speech therapy lasted for three weeks and the physical therapy six weeks. I saw the nurse each Friday, the physical therapist came twice per week, and the physical therapist came twice per week, while the speech therapist came once per week for three weeks.

It was my hope then, that I'd never, have to face learning to walk again in my life! I dreaded physical therapy sessions. Fear enveloped my entire being each time the sessions drew near. Despite the fear, however, I had to muster the courage and do the exercises.

I had a choice—I had painted in my mind, two pictures: one sitting and moving around in a wheelchair for the rest of my life and the other, seeing myself walking as I used to. The latter really resonated with me. I couldn't give up! There was no time to call it quits! I must walk again! And by God's grace, it was going to happen!

I had to learn how to use my fine and gross motor skills all over again. Learning to balance on one leg to the next was very scary, but

I had to do it! I also had to relearn how to coordinate the rest of my body with moving my feet.

Every time I stepped on the wooden floor, my feet went plop! plop! plop! You could hear the timidity in each step I made. I would often refer to myself as "Big Foot". The therapist walked on my left side, holding my left hand, providing support. The focus was balancing—eye, hand, and feet coordination. As we moved along, she counted in increments of tens. I'd walk back and forth in the passage that led from my bedroom to my bathroom.

I was born a lefthander and after the aneurysm my right hand wanted to take over as the dominant hand. My right hand would automatically weaponized objects. It was so bad that I'd to use my left hand to keep my right hand under control. To get the throwing of objects to cease, I'd to do a lot of positive self-talk.

To get me through these repetitive sessions, I had to rely on the Word of God. From memory, I would mumble under my breath as I learned the art of walking: "Not by might, nor by power, but by My Spirit," Says the Lord of hosts" (Zech. 4:6, NKJV); "Perfect love casts out fear, because fear involves torment" (1 John 4:18, NKJV); and "For God has not given us the spirit of fear, but of power, and of love, and of a sound mind" (2 Tim. 1:7, NKJV).

I realized it wasn't going to be easy. I was so afraid! So, with much prayer, repeated promises from the Bible, a lot of positive self-talk, and receiving encouragement and support from the folks around me, I pressed on. There was no time to lose hope. I knew I wasn't alone. Not once did God let me go or His promises ever failed!

It was now the beginning of December, 2011, and I really thought by then I'd be walking and be back at work. However, my hope of returning to work was dashed when I made my second visit to the neurosurgeon. It was then that I found out that my road to recovery was going to be a long, long one. There was no light at the end of the tunnel for me. Not yet, and I didn't know when!

There were days when the physical therapy sessions went well and other days when it felt like a complete failure. I wanted to call it quits. There were times I had to do some serious positive self-talk. My husband Wendell and my mother, Iris were my cheerleaders and number one fans. Despite the struggles, they kept saying, "You gotta do it! Come on, you can do it! My therapists eventually joined my husband and mother as my cheerleaders. It was the same with my speech therapy sessions.

My mother, my caregiver during the day, kept encouraging me with promises from the Bible. She actually wrote two of her favorite promises and gave them to me, "Heal me O Lord, and I shall be healed; save me, and I shall be saved, for thou art my praise" (Jer. 17:14, KJV).

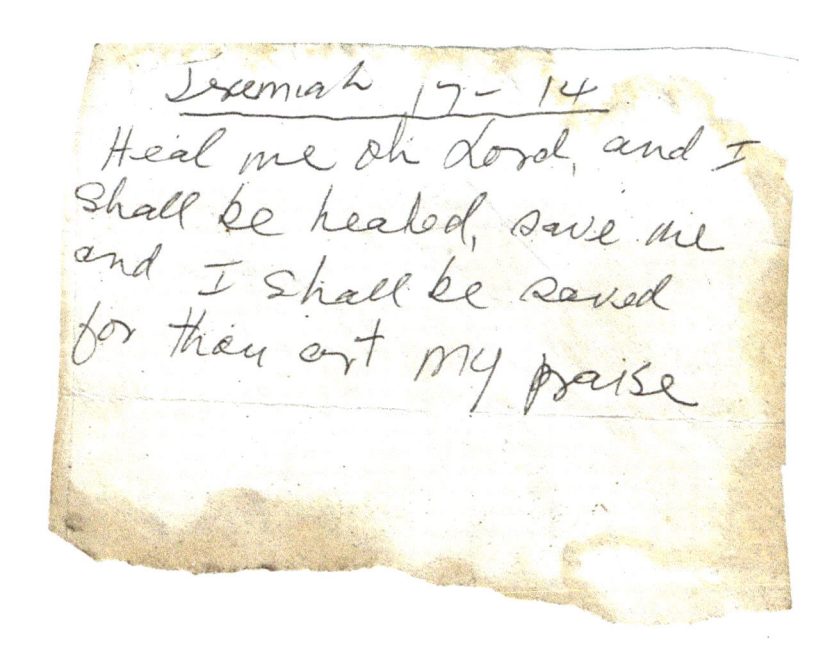

And, "Let my mouth be filled with thy praise and with thy honor all the day" (Ps. 71:8, KJV).

> Psalm 71-8
> Let my mouth be
> filled with thy praise
> and with thy honour
> all the day

Relying on optics to build my faith, I instead replaced optics with trusting God. I truly believed at the time, that my relationship with God was severely tested. It was just God and me.

The sessions with the speech therapist were pleasant. I was still unable to sit up and do the speech exercises. I did the exercises lying on my back in bed. The exercises consisted of making faces, swallowing, opening and closing my mouth, inhaling and exhaling, enunciation and pronunciation of words with double letters and one to three syllable words. *Repetition! Repetition! Repetition! Practice! Practice! Practice!* However, I soon realized that I was using words out of context. I'd find myself saying, "The plate is in the chicken" when it should have been "The plate is in the kitchen." This went on for quite some time, and even today there are times when this still occurs. I sometimes used sin for skin, incriminate for discriminate, disappointed for disappeared, play for pray, medication for meditation, and so on. By this time my outpatient Visiting Nursing Service program ended but I was still having issues pertaining to my sight, speech and walking. I was still unable to balance, coordinate, and walk the way I used to. What would be next? I wanted to walk! Was this the end? By any means necessary, it was going to happen! Not in my time, but I *know* that I *know* that I *know* it would happen in the time appointed by God! Trust, waiting, and patience were three virtues I learned during this time.

After the outpatient services ended, Dr. Kadine was instrumental in arranging for me to see a speech pathologist. She did some tests to find out if my receptive and expressive language skills were affected by the brain aneurysm. After chewing a few graham cracker cookies, the speech therapist instructed me to drink from a small plastic cup small amounts of water. At the end of the session, I was told that my swallowing was good and as time went on, my receptive and expressive language skills would improve. I left the speech pathologist's office feeling optimistic about my speech and language abilities.

But there was another cause for concern. After leaving the rehab facility, one day, I noticed while lying in bed that something wasn't right with my right ear. I wasn't hearing. So, I made an appointment to see an ear, nose, and throat specialist. On my visit to see the ENT specialist, I underwent a thorough evaluation. He requested the audiologists on site to do a comprehensive evaluation of my hearing. She escorted me to an enclosed room.

On entering the room, I noticed in the center a soft, black chair. It was a small room and there was a sound of silence. If a pin dropped you could hear it. That's how quiet it was. In one of the corners in the room, was a table with toys of many different shapes and sizes. From what I'd observed, I came to the conclusion that adults and children alike were evaluated in that tiny space. I didn't know what to expect. As a special education teacher, I was acquainted with the

Frequency Modulation (FM) machine because I'd used it as an assistive device to teach children who were hearing impaired.

It was the first time I was seeing an Audiometer machine. However, I knew that it was used to measure hearing. The audiologist invited me to sit in the black armchair. Then, before the testing began, the Audiologist told me that she was going to have me listen to some sounds. And if I heard the sounds, I should press a button on a remote she gave me. After she explained the procedure, she left the room. The testing began with the right ear. As the test progressed, I was hearing soft and loud sounds, or so I'd thought. The testing of the left ear followed and I also heard soft and loud sounds. After the testing was completed, I learned that I had completely lost the earring in my right ear. Another curve ball came and stole yet another base from me. On hearing the news, I didn't display how I was feeling on the outside, but on the inside my heart was drowning in tears. Tears of disappointment and discouragement.

On my way home, I kept saying to myself, "This could not be, it could not be true." This was too much for me to digest, so I decided to seek two other opinions. And of course the loss of hearing in my right ear was confirmed. I'd to find solace in the Word of God. My world was literally falling apart. "Whenever I'm afraid, I'll trust in you" (Ps. 56:3, NKJV). This verse from the Bible was now a reality. How could I trust God when my world was falling apart? I still believed and had hoped that my hearing was going to return with time.

Now I was taking the inflammatory drug Prednisone "the miracle drug" and the epileptic drug Keppra. I took the Prednisone for seven days but continued taking the Keppra. Cornmeal porridge and pigeon peas were the foods that I ate before I swallowed the tablets prescribed. How relieved I felt when the final day came to pop the last Predisone. To this day I cannot bear the sight of cornmeal porridge and pigeon peas soup. Enough was enough!

After the seven days were over, I went for a follow-up visit to the ENT specialist. The outcome remained the same. About a month after, I felt sick and decided to go to the emergency room. I happened to have taken the prescription bottle with the Keppra tablets with me. I showed the bottle to the attending physician, and after an evaluation, the decision was made for me to discontinue taking Keppra.

Some years back, as a freshman in college and a new believer in Jesus Christ, I heard for the first time the song "Will Your Anchor Hold in the Storms of Life?" Years had passed, and now the song came back to my mind. I'd to face this question and live out the words of the song in my life. At the time, I felt like a ship, caught in a severe storm at sea. I felt like the ship, I was going under. Then I remembered the story in the Bible with Jesus and His disciples on a boat caught in a severe storm. Jesus was fast asleep on the boat when the disciples became afraid. They became hopeless. They needed help. Then, they remembered the Master of the ocean, sea and sky, sleeping somewhere in the boat. They realized that He was the only one who could help them out of the trouble they were facing. So they went to Him for help.

I felt like the disciples. When they found Jesus, they got the help they needed. Jesus said, "Peace! Be still!" (Mark 4:39, KJV). I accepted my situation, and realized I couldn't go it alone. I needed help. I felt like I was drowning in my circumstances. My health, finances, career, you name it, were all going under. I was quickly going under emotionally.

Every day, my entire life flashed before me. The picture wasn't a pleasant one. It was getting bleaker and bleaker. In my mind, I thought I wouldn't make it, so I cried out to Jesus for the help I needed because I was sure I was going under. I would search my brain for promises that I'd memorized and stored over the years that would help me cope. I'd repeat these promises silently every day. I needed something to keep my mind at peace. And sure enough, I found these promises all filed away in my brain: "You will keep him in perfect peace, Whose mind is stayed on You, Because he trusts in You" (Isa. 26:3, NKJV). "Peace I leave with you, My peace I give to you; not as the world give do I give to you. Let not your heart be troubled, neither let it be afraid" (John 14:27, NKJV). "Great peace have those who love Your law, And nothing causes them to stumble" (Ps.119:165, NKJV).

There was one particular promise that kept going over and over in my mind. "For he shall be as a tree planted by the waters, and that spreadeth out her roots by the river, and shall not see when heat cometh, but her leaf shall be green; and shall not be careful in the year of drought, neither shall cease from yielding fruit" (Jer. 17:8, KJV). Every day as I lay in bed on my back, Jeremiah 17:8 kept playing like a recorded message over and over in my head. Then one day, while looking through the large front window of my bedroom (I began calling the bedroom "a room with a view"), while staring at the blue canopy, it was as if someone was explaining to me the meaning of the verse of scripture. *"You have found yourself between a rock and a hard place in your life, and you need to see yourself as a tree. Your faith is like the roots of that tree. You need to anchor your faith in God. You must trust God no matter the outcome."*

Another day, while looking through the same window, I heard a soft voice saying to me, "For my thoughts are not your thoughts, Nor are your ways My ways, saith the Lord. For as the heavens are higher than the earth, So are My ways higher than your ways, and My thoughts than your thoughts" (Isa. 55:8-9 NKJV). Everywhere

I turned, doors seemed to slam in my face. I felt like a caged bird. Beaten up, neglected, and made fun of.

Before my illness, I'd read my Bible, but not in depth. I knew most of the stories from my childhood, but I never spent quality time in the Word. However, I still believed then, and I still do now, that the mornings I spent during my working years, riding the train to work, (approximately forty minutes) reading the Bible, was the platform that the Holy Spirit used to build my faith.

Each morning, I'd focused on different Bible characters: the problems they faced and the solutions God revealed to them. I became fascinated with the various ways God chose to intervene in the lives of each character. Every now and then, I'd supplement reading the Bible with a devotional book, a spiritual memoir, or an inspirational magazine. I loved a good read. Later on, I included journaling to this activity.

Reading these materials were beneficial for me. It was then that I got insight on how each character, like Moses, Joshua, Job, David, Gideon, Isaiah, Jeremiah, Naomi, Ruth, Hagar, Nehemiah, dealt with suffering and pain and the impact pain and suffering had on them. In addition, my take away from reading each story was that the characters never lost hope. I learned that in the midst of suffering, pain, and other life-threatening challenges, Jesus was their *only* answer.

I randomly selected and read some of the miracle stories Jesus performed in the first four books of the New Testament. It was while reading the gospels I saw when Jesus met people, whether it was an individual, a multitude, a believer, nonbeliever, an outcast, Jew or Gentile, He first catered to their physical needs before focusing on the spiritual. I also realized that Jesus spent most of His time doing more healing than teaching and preaching.

Meeting the spiritual and physical needs of the people were very important to Jesus. I read also that Jesus spent time praying. Prayer was very important to Him and played a major role in His life. Yes, I did pray. Yes, it was a part of my lifestyle, *but* I was not intentional about it. I'd prayed many prayers before my illness and certainly got answers, whether it was yes, no, or wait. But it was in the month of November 2011 that my prayer life took on a new meaning. Prayer became the foremost pillar of my faith. You see, I was the beneficiary of the outcome of personal and intercessory prayers. Prayer became more real to me.

In high school and college, I developed a love for literature and history. I was very fascinated with characters in secular stories. As I read secular stories I saw that the story elements were similar to ones in the Bible. On reading the Bible, I'd focused on the characters, settings, problems, and solutions without seriously giving a thought to the spiritual applications. The more I read, some of the stories sounded like the soap operas of our day, but there was more to be gained from a spiritual aspect.

Keeping my mind focused on the Lord was sometimes a struggle. It wasn't a walk over. I had to rely on the Holy Spirit for guidance and help. Humanly, this was impossible. So, I decided to compile an anthology of spiritual songs, a mix of traditional and contemporary songs and this I added to my arsenal against the tormentor and enemy of souls. There were several songs that helped me get through this nightmare. One of them was "Fear Not Tomorrow, God is Already There" authored by Carolyn Adkins and sung by the Collingsworth family, *(permission granted)*.

Fear Not Tomorrow, God is Already There

In the age of uncertainty, questions comes to my mind.
What is waiting ahead for me and the rest of mankind.
Fear not tomorrow, God is already there.
He's charting the course you take.
He sees each hidden snare.
He's waiting to guide you through each burden and care.
Fear not tomorrow, God is already there.

Are you troubled o'er things to come?
Is your future unsure?
And are you dreading the coming dawn? A long day to endure?
Fear not tomorrow, God is already there.
He's charting the course you take.
He sees each hidden snare.
He's waiting to guide you through each burden and care
Fear not tomorrow, God is already there.

Many things about tomorrow I don't seem to understand.
Oh, but I know Who holds tomorrow.
And I know, oh, I know
Yes, I know Who holds my hand
Fear not tomorrow, God is already there.
Already there.

"For God hath not given us the spirit of fear; but of power, and of love, and of a sound mind" (2 Tim. 1:7, KJV).

Fear or Faith?

The therapy sessions called for a lot of effort on my part to do the exercises. Fear took over, especially when it came time for me to do physical therapy. I never looked forward to these sessions. Leaving the comfort of my bed was not something I looked forward to do. After each session I was completely therapy, twice per week, physical therapy, twice per week, and a visiting nurse. The therapy sessions called for a lot of effort on my part to do the exercises. Fear took over, especially when it came time for me to do physical therapy. I never looked forward to these sessions. Leaving the comfort of my bed was not something I looked forward to do.

Each time, fear got the better of me. Learning to walk again was very scary, and even more, extremely challenging, especially for an adult my age. No wonder God in His wisdom made us learn to walk at the toddler stage of our lives. It was the scariest thing I'd ever done in my life. It was as if I never walked before. Each time I would try to leave my bed, I would be gripped with fear. Two monsters showed up—*vertigo and tinnitus*!

My head would spin and spin. And it seemed that the room was also spinning. There was no slowing down. I became so fearful. I had to find a way to deal with this phenomenon. I had to do something. As the days went by, fear began to overpower me. I was being crippled by it. And if I gave it the chance, fear would have the ability, to control, and to cause hopelessness and a lack of trust in God. I told God how I was feeling and how scared I was. He had to let this bitter experience pass from me.

One day, out of the clear blue, I found myself repeating promises from the Bible. "For God has not given us the spirit of fear, but of power and of love, and of a sound mind" (2 Tim. 1:7 NKJV)."I can do all things through Christ who strengthens me" (Phil. 4:13,

NKJV). "'Not by might, nor by power, but by my Spirit,' says the Lord of hosts" (Zech. 4:6, NKJV). I repeated these three promises each time I placed my feet on the floor to take the first step.

Repetition, repetition, repetition became a part of my routine. This behavior lasted for approximately three months until one day I slowly got up, placed one foot on the floor, and realized that the walls of the room weren't spinning and closing in on me anymore. Victory was mine! I claimed victory in Jesus' name! I was an overcomer. All fear had disappeared. I was freed from the shackle of fear. I had learned from the experience that fear can become a monster.

It was in the second week of this outpatient service that an occupational therapists showed up at my home. The moment had presented itself for me to demonstrate to him that I wasn't in need of his service. So, I volunteered to write and undo the buttons on the blouse I was wearing, just to demonstrate to him that I didn't need occupational therapy. He watched as I executed the tasks he requested of me. Then he said; "You're right; you really don't need my service after all!" And that was it! Out the front door he went, never to be seen again!

The days gingerly danced on. I was trying desperately to walk again. There were times when I looked at my emaciated body in the mirror and cried (I was now weighing a measly eighty-five pounds, a descent from a healthy looking 130-pound female). I was in total shock! I questioned, was this really me? I had to keep my focus on God.

One night, while lying in bed, I reached for my Bible laying on the night table, and for some reason it opened to the book Habakkuk, to be exact chapter 2. Suddenly mine eyes zeroed on verse 3 "For the vision is yet for an appointed time; but at the end it shall speak, and not lie: though it tarry, wait for it; because it will surely come, it will not tarry" (Hab. 2:3, NKJV).

I kept reading the verse over and over again. Was the Holy Spirit trying to tell me something regarding my future and my circumstance? It was then that I made the decision to spend time trying to put meaning to some of the words I'd read in the verse, words such as *vision, yet, appointed, time, end, wait, surely, come,* and *tarry*.

The word *vision* was familiar to me because I'd read about characters in the Bible like Daniel, Cornelius the Centurion, Peter, Paul, and John on the Isle of Patmos having visions. I'd also heard of contemporary individuals having visions. But what did vision had to do with me? First, I wanted to know the difference between a vision and a dream.

So, the first thing I did was to look at some definitions given by my old Oxford dictionary, the Webster, and of course a Thesaurus. I even googled the words. From what I'd researched, I came up with a definition for myself. My definition of a vision: A vision happens when one is wide awake, and a dream takes place while one is asleep.

For once, I wasn't aware of the magnitude of the situation I was facing, how my life would never be the same again. However, as the days turned into weeks and weeks into months, I'd slowly grasped the reality that my life had changed not for a day, but forever. The impact was truly great. I believed that I was going to be able to walk again and as the verse said it was going to be at an appointed time. I took that to have meant a special time, a time when God would act. Things would begin to happen! But I'd to wait. In the meantime, I'd to trust God. I'd to develop the virtues of patience and waiting for God to be God—in His own time and way. I had my own time line, and God had His.

My timeline saw me getting back to work in a few weeks time. But my time line was wrong. To how things were working out, my calculation was really off. As time went on, I realized I wouldn't be going back to work anytime soon. As the days progressed, I realized that it was all left up to God. He also reminded me of this fact when I read what the psalmist David wrote: "My times are in your hands" (Ps. 31:15, KJV). *Waiting* was the name of the game. I'd to wait on the Lord and watch as the vision happened. I was going to walk again!

My face was literally twisted, and my mouth was now situated at the top of my forehead. The right side of my face was numb. I was soon to discover I was dealing with facial paralysis and drooping. I could only feel the left side of my scalp and not the right side. I felt like tiny ants were crawling constantly up and down the right side of my face, not to mention my lips.

This felt like a nerve problem. Sometimes, the right side of my face would twitch, at all times my chin and right ear were numb to the touch. I'd be stuck with a sharp object and wouldn't know it because of the numbness. I would feel the numbness on and off in my left fingers and toes. The only time I didn't have the antsy feeling in my face and the numbness in my left fingers and toes was when I was asleep. The moment I opened my eyes, the sensations would immediately return. I often referred to it as my "*invisible hell.*"

Approximately twenty years ago I'd to undergo an emergency retinal surgery. This was due to a detached retina in my right eye. It began one afternoon when I returned home from work that I noticed after throwing a piece of paper in the kitchen trash bin, on raising my head I was seeing from my right eye the color prism. I began to rub my eye thinking that the colors would go away. But nothing changed. I blinked several times and still there was no change. It was then that I realized that something was wrong with my eye. I immediately reached for the house phone, and proceeded to call a church sister who lived a few blocks away. I told her what had happened and that I was on my way to the hospital. That evening she volunteered to take me to the hospital. And that was when the nightmare began to reattach the retina in my right eye.

After the first surgery, for approximately six weeks I lived in a world of darkness. I wasn't able to see from the right eye. It was as black as night, I just had to trust God and pray that my sight would eventually returned, which it eventually did. Early one Friday morning, the fifth week after the retina surgery, I was standing at the front door of my home when I suddenly realized that I was seeing the color of our red car parked at the gate.

I was so excited that I shared the experience with my husband. To be sure that it was not a figment of my imagination, I looked across at our neighbor's house, and saw that the sun had risen and had cast its rays on the front window of the house. I glanced twice. Could it be real? I was seeing glimmers of light from the sun shining on the window. My sight was on its way back! I was so happy.

Shortly after the vision returned in the right eye, I developed an infection. Due to the infection, I lost my sight again. A year later I'd to undergo a second surgery. An artificial lens was then used to replace the lens I was born with. It was a scary time, especially when after the first surgery, the doctor told me that there was no guarantee that the vision in my right eye would return.

Coupled with the retinal detachment a few years back, and now after the brain aneurysm I developed more issues with my vision. Now both eyes had become very much off-focused, especially the right one. Over the right eye were layers of dead skin that looked like tiny fish scales. Four years later, in March of 2015, the time came for me to change my glasses and to be checked for glaucoma. So, I went to an Optometrist. After the tests were completed, it was then discovered that the pressure in both eyes measured 35 mm Hg. The normal pressure ranges from 10—21 mm Hg. He educated me on the danger of having such high pressure in my eyes. He insisted that I immediately see a retina specialist.

I'd heard the word *glaucoma* before, and that's all I knew but never knew of the danger. I left the optometrist's office with a sense of urgency and fear, wobbling on my cane, which had become one of my dearest friends. I didn't know at the time why there was such urgency until I began researching and reading literature on retinal detachment and other eye diseases. From my reading, I learned that several trauma to the eye could cause the pressure to be elevated. For several years, I'd been under the care of a retina specialist due to a retinal detachment in the right eye.

Over the years I've prayed many prayers, but the fear of becoming blind made my prayers more urgent and meaningful. The evening hours passed, and I retired to bed. I slept through the night. Then morning came. Around the usual time, my prayer partner Sister "Eddy" called me on the phone. It was prayer time. First, as usual, we greeted each other before we prayed. Next, as was our norm, we commented on a news issue of the morning and discussed the devotional for the day. The last thing we did each morning was pray. It was during our conversational time that I told my prayer partner about the outcome of my visit the day before to the optometrist.

It was then that I asked her if she knew of an ophthalmologist that I could see. At the time I didn't know that she was seeing one. She answered in the affirmative and after we prayed, she gave me the telephone number. After I got off the telephone, without hesitation, I dialed the number. I quickly explained what I was about to the person on the other end of the line and she gave me an appointment to see the ophthalmologist for 10 o'clock the following Tuesday.

I called my prayer partner and told her that I'd gotten an appointment. She was amazed and exclaimed, "It's very difficult to get appointments so quickly with this doctor. The wait list is normally a very long one." I took note of what she'd said, and right there and then, I took it as a sign that God was on my case.

It took forever for the next Tuesday to arrive. However, Tuesday finally arrived. So, off I went to see the ophthalmologist. Sure enough the pressure in both eyes measured 35 mm Hg. I was told that I was at high risk for glaucoma. I had to get the pressure down. Since then, every night I had to religiously put the medication prescribed in both eyes. At the start of the treatment, I was just fine administering the drops in my eyes. Then one morning a few months afterward, I could hardly opened up both eyes. The pain I felt was so excruciating that I had to slowly force them open. That morning, I called Alberto who was kind enough to take me to the eye clinic at the hospital to see an ophthalmologist.

After describing how I was feeling, the doctor added an over-the-counter nighttime ointment, along with a day time ointment, to be used with the prescribed eye medication, Latanoprost at nights. This led to the pressure readings in my eyes decreasing to 14 mm Hg. To this day I sometimes struggle in the mornings to open up my eyes because of severe pain, despite administering the drops and ointment. At other times, the right eye would suddenly become red and would take a good while for the redness to disappear.

My ability to produce tears from the right eye was lost due to the injury of the optic nerves because of the brain aneurysm. When I did cry, it was the left eye that did the crying. It was as if the right eye had forgotten that producing tears was one of its jobs. There were instances where my right eye would be red as fire. Looking at me, one would have thought that I was in a fight and got punched in it. At nights, I'd to wear a patch over the right eye to keep it closed while I was asleep.

For approximately five years, I took the prescribed eye drop Latanoprost and continued to take the over the counter lubricant for dryness. Since then, after undergoing surgery on my left eye, the eye drop Dorzolamide Hel-timol was added. However, the latter was changed to Brimonidine Tartrate. And every three months onwards, I was subjected to a battery of field vision and retina tests.

My sense of smell in my right nostril was very much gone; this was due to the numbness on the right side of my face. The outer part of my nose felt hard like a stone. It felt like some strange object was stuck in it, which prevented me from smelling and breathing properly. I had to get used to this change in feeling, smelling, and breathing. I was only breathing from my left nostril. This condition led to several bouts of sinus infections. Off again I went to see another ENT specialist.

My taste buds were now in the reverse mode. My ability to enjoy food was no more. I only ate food to stay alive. Foods that were sour were now sweet to the taste, and no matter what kind of food it was, my tongue like a detective was able to find the salt. Although, I'd never had hypertensive issues before I got ill, now I had to be extra careful with my salt intake. My blood pressure readings remained within the normal range. There was never a dull moment, every day there was always something new happening or a new discovery.

It was at sunset on New Year's Eve 2016 that I felt a lump on the right side of my throat. So, I stuck my left index finger down my throat to retrieve what it was, that was causing me discomfort. I used my finger to pull the object up. The object slowly slid on my tongue and flew on to a piece of tissue I was holding in my right hand. Startled, I held the object up close and examined it. I saw that it was several rice grains hugging each other tightly with help from my saliva. It was in the shape of a ball.

In the days that followed, I kept feeling the sensation in my throat. There were times when I felt as if I was suffocating. Questions kept coming to my mind. Could I have choked on the rice ball? Did the rice ball formed in my esophagus and gradually worked itself up to my throat? I was of the opinion that eating several meals that consisted of rice over a period of time had led to several grains creating the ball. After the incident, I stopped eating rice for a while. Instead I ate root foods like yams and potatoes.

Throughout this ordeal, I had to depend solely on Jesus and Jesus only. At times I felt like a caged bird. Where could I go? Through it all, I decided that I would never asked God why? In my opinion, me asking God for an answer would only have me cast doubt on His sovereignty. Whenever I was tempted to ask God why, I immediately dismissed it from my mind.

Trusting God, and taking Him at His Word, that when He said, "And we know that all things work together for good to them that love God, to them who are the called according to his purpose" (Rom. 8:28, KJV), He meant it. It might not be good right now, but in the end it would work out for my good. This was a hard pill to swallow, but in the end I had to see God as intentional.

Still, no income was forthcoming. In the meantime while struggling with my health, we lived on one salary. My leave was in chaos. Everywhere I turned for help it was just confusion. While lying in bed on my back, I worked the phone. I reached out for help wherever I could get it. I was determined to get help!

The first place I decided to call for help was the Human Resources section of the Department of Education. It was then that I found out that they'd in fact received the paperwork for my leave application, but they were unable to process it, due to missing signatures. Next, I called the secretary of the school I'd worked and told her of the problem.

Then she requested that I resend the copies of the original documents to her, so she could resubmit it to the district office for the missing signatures to be added. I waited approximately a month and still there was no word on my sick leave application.

Again, I reached out to the Human Resources section of the Department of Education. This time I was told that they'd received the signed documents. But I also needed my neurologists to fill out another set of papers and submit same to the department as soon as possible (which by the way I never received), and returned it to the Human Resources Section.

After two days, I finally received the new documents in the mail. I was just going back and forth, getting no clear answers. I now felt like a number on a page. No answers were forthcoming, and of course, and to top it off, I wasn't receiving any remuneration. Each time a new document was requested and had to be submitted for my leave to be authorized. However, when all of that was taking place, I knew that God was with me. I'd read in my Bible more than once that, "No weapon that is formed against thee shall prosper" (Isa. 54:17, KJV). I had full assurance that God was looking out for me. He had my back! I truly believed that He did. He said in His Word, "I will never leave you, nor forsake you" (Heb. 13:5, NKJV). And, "Many are the afflictions of the righteous, But the Lord delivers him out of them all" (Ps. 34:19, NKJV).

Everywhere I turned it was as if a door slammed shut in my face. I can clearly recall an incident that took place over the telephone. I was trying to find out where in the pipeline my application for sabbatical leave was with a union representative who accused me of shouting at her. Which I never did. The brain aneurysm had also affected my speech, and even the sound of my voice. I tried explaining to her why my voice sounded the way it did, but she just didn't want to hear it. I wasn't given the time to explain what was happening; the lady proceeded to tell me to fax her the copies of the paper pertaining to my case. I wasn't looking for any sympathy from her. I just needed help.

At the end of the call, I felt so dejected, abused, beaten up, broken, and hopeless that I began to cry. Before I got off the phone, I was given a fax number and told to fax all the paperwork pertaining to my leave application. To end this horrible call, I said goodbye, and hung up the phone. The next day, I asked a friend to fax the leave application forms as I was instructed to do. I waited for two weeks to hear from this individual before calling to find out if anything was done. At first, I hesitated to call, but after two weeks, I eventually mustered up the courage and made the call.

I greeted the woman on the other side of the line with a cheery good morning as best as I could have said it. Next, I introduced myself, beginning with my name, and gave the reason why I was calling. Then she told me she hadn't received the leave application forms that she said I was to fax to her. I didn't say another word. All I heard was; "Please fax them to me again." At her request, I did fax the forms a second time to her, and that was the end of that story.

After that episode, I decided to reach out at the time to the union representative at the school where I'd worked. I left several messages on her voicemail, but she never returned my calls. Shortly after, an election was held and a new union representative was elected. One day while lying in bed, the phone rang. I picked up the receiver and heard a familiar voice. The person on the other end was the new union chapter leader at the school.

By then, the staff had been informed of my illness. So, I didn't have to go into much details. I told her of the difficulties I was experiencing in getting my paperwork through the system. It was then that she promised to be my voice, hands, and feet. That was that. I never heard from her again. Her election as union representative didn't move the needle any further. My case remained as it was, and every day while lying in bed, I worked the telephone to get some assistance. On my own and with the help of God, I was still trying to get answers, and none was forthcoming, yet I was not about to throw in the towel.

I fell ill on October 8, 2011. It was now January 2012. Still no word regarding my sick leave being approved. My union office was situated in the borough where I worked, so it would've been difficult for me to go there because of my mobility issues. Then Thelma F., a member of my community of faith and also a teacher, suggested and volunteered to take me to the union office in the borough where I lived because of its close proximity to my home. At the time when this took place, I began making baby steps. I was able to push myself and, with my friend's help, made it to her car.

Thelma F. drove me to the union office where I met a union representative. I gave her copies of my sick leave application and left shortly after. That was also the end of that story. I had to be proactive, persistent, resilient, and patient. But more than all, I had to *trust* God. I made calls day in, day out, and wasn't getting anywhere. Everything was at a standstill. Then, finally one day after making repeated calls, a breakthrough came.

I believed that the Holy Spirit made an impression on me to call the main office of the teacher's union. I took up the telephone and dialed one of many numbers I had before me at the time. On the other end of the call, I heard a friendly voice. I sheepishly gave my name and began to tell the reason for calling. As I proceeded to tell her my reason for calling, out of the clear blue, the lady said to me in my one ear, "I'm familiar with your case."

She told me that she had spoken to my husband while I was hospitalized and instructed him what papers should be filed for me to make the application for sick leave. Somehow, God in His infinite wisdom, caused me to choose a telephone number at random, which

Road to Recovery Continues at Home

led me to the same individual who was already familiar with my case from the onset of my illness. Someone was looking out for me. Sure enough, I was beginning to understand what Exod. 14:14, (NKJV) truly meant: "The Lord will fight for you, and you shall hold your peace."

Now, I had found another angel. At the time, the lady was a retiree and was a volunteer at the union office. She only went into the office on Tuesdays and Thursdays, and in our conversation, she told me that in future if I had questions, she would gladly answer them. And if she couldn't, she'd find someone who could. This was my life line after going through a maze of ups and downs, twists, and turns.

I continued spending my days reading my Bible, devotional books, journaling, praying really hard, and working the telephone. There were times I felt as if I was working a phone bank. Sometimes I would see a glimmer of light at the end of the tunnel. Then the light would slowly fade away, and I was right back to square one.

I was still unable to do business on my own due to immobility. However, again I remembered the promise, "The Lord will fight for you, and you shall hold your peace" (Exod. 14: 14, NKJV). I soon came to the conclusion that in His time, God would show up! In the fullness of time, He'd put the missing parts of the puzzle together. In the meantime, I continued doing several therapy sessions. Each day, my trust in God, hope in God, and patience was growing stronger. I spent many quiet hours reflecting on the goodness of God and the passionate love that He had towards me.

Humanly, sometimes I found it difficult to digest what was happening to me, but even in the darkest of times, God showed up in subtle ways, just when it seemed that hope was fading. He would reassure me that He was with me and my future was in His hand. In my mind's eye I saw myself literally walking as I did before I became ill. As the days went by; however, I realized that this would only happen on God's time, not on my time. I had no doubt it was going to come; there was an appointed time for it to happen. My entire body would be restored to what it used to be.

"Whenever I'm afraid, I'll trust in You"
(Psalms 56:3 NKJV).

Vertigo! Tinnitus!

I was making steady progress, or so I thought when out of the clear blue I was faced with another challenge—Vertigo. I was now sitting up in bed for longer periods, although I still had to use two pillows to support my back. However, I really thought I was getting my groove back. Slowly, I was taking small steps. Day by day, my steps became more frequent, and as I walked on the stairs, my stomach would rumble like a volcano ready to erupt. This went on for some time until one day I realized that when I placed my feet on the floor, the room would be spinning like a top. It seemed as if the four walls of the room were caving in on me. I realized that I was experiencing vertigo. I'd heard about it, but experiencing it, never!

The vertigo continued for days, going into weeks, weeks turning into months. Each time I made the attempt to get up from my bed, I had to quote scriptures to keep fear away. I still had to get up and do the walking exercises, but the vertigo kept attacking me. I thought this monster would immediately go away, but it seemed it had come to stay forever. It got so unbearable that I had to cry out to God for deliverance. Each time I attempted to walk, I felt like I was going into a deep hole. Finally, after much prayer, support, and encouragement from my husband and mother, and with persistency and resiliency, I finally got a breakthrough!

Slowly, I was taking small steps. Day by day, my steps became more frequent, and as I walked on the stairs, my stomach would rumble like a volcano ready to erupt. This went on for some time until one day I realized that when I placed my feet on the floor, the room would be spinning like a top. I realized that I was experiencing vertigo. I'd heard about it, but experiencing it, never! The vertigo continued for days, going into weeks, weeks turning into months. Each time I made the attempt to get up from my bed, I had to quote scriptures to keep fear away. It seemed as if the four walls of the room were caving in on me.

It was a cool spring night in April, 2019, and I was on the house telephone when I heard a beeping sound coming. It sounded like a vital sign machine. I was on the call for approximately thirty minutes when I heard a small voice instructing me to immediately end the call and put the telephone back into its cradle.

I obeyed. Since the aneurysm, I'd completely lost the hearing in my right ear. So, I'd tried protecting the hearing in my left ear. I did exactly what I was told to do and got ready for bed. And off to sleep I went. I slept very soundly as usual that night. However, when morning came and I opened mine eyes, I heard the beeping of the vital signs machine from the night before and it seemed like it was coming from my head. Over and over it went, nonstop! I felt like I was losing my mind. I used my hands and placed pressure next to both ears hoping that the ringing would go away. But it didn't.

I cried aloud, "God, where are You?" "I've already lost hearing in one ear and now this!" "You have to help me!" I felt as if someone was persistently beating me nonstop in my head. It became unbearable. I swung my head to the left, then to the right, thinking that I would've gotten rid of the sound. But to no avail. I kept praying. I was petrified. But during this ordeal I just kept crying and praying. I couldn't imagine myself living with this for the rest of my life.

For a long time, my tears flowed that morning. And the more I prayed! And in my tearful, prayer moment, the promise "And it shall come to pass, that before they call, I will answer, and while they are yet speaking, I will hear" (Isa. 65:24, KJV) came to mind. All of a sudden, I heard a loud pop in my left ear, and there was stillness. God had heard my prayers, seen my tears, and saw the state my heart was in. I was so grateful to God for tending to my cry immediately. After my bout with tinnitus, I researched the subject. From the literature I'd read, tinnitus would go away on its own. It could take weeks, months, or years for it to go. However, to live with that constant ringing in my ears was maddening for me. I thank God that He heard my cry for help that morning and delivered me immediately from my torture.

I wanted to know what caused the ringing in my ears. So, I took to the internet. I entered "ringing sound in my ear" in the browser and the word tinnitus appeared. I saw several websites, but I chose to visit WebMD. According to Dr. Minesh Khatri:

> "Tinnitus (pronounced ti-ni-tus), or ringing in the ears, is the sensation of hearing ringing, buzzing, hissing, chirping, whistling, or other sounds. The noise can be intermittent or continuous, and can vary in loudness. It is often worse when background noise is low, so you may be most aware of it at night when you're trying to fall asleep in a quiet room. In rare cases, the sound beats in sync with your heart (pulsatile tinnitus)....
>
> Prolonged exposure to loud sounds is the most common cause of tinnitus. Up to 90% of people with tinnitus have some level of noise-induced hearing loss. The noise causes permanent damage to the sound-sensitive cells of the cochlea, a spiral-shaped organ in the inner ear. Kharti, Minesh, MD. 'Understanding Tinnitus--the Basics', medically reviewed on November 12, 2019, viewed on 18 November, 2021, http://www.webmd.com>

Every night at eight o'clock, the Hope Channel, a religious channel would air a nightly program titled *Let's Pray* and with bated breath I would eagerly wait to watch. I would sit back on my pillow and watched and listened from one ear (by this it was official; I'd completely lost the hearing in my right ear). Night after night as I listened, and watched, I became encouraged. I was soon to realize there were other individuals within the faith community, who were also experiencing severe hardships and trials, in particular, health challenges.

I realized that I wasn't alone. There were individuals who called a week or two before requesting prayer for whatever they deemed as giants in their lives. When a prayer was answered, it was celebrated by the faith community and was called a "praise report." The program presenters soon became my friends in television land and expanded to the wider community of believers. Although I didn't know these people, I added them to my support group. I really felt a part of the group. They didn't know me, and neither did I know them, but I still felt that I belonged. I felt as if they were feeling my hurt and pain, and I was doing the same for them.

One night in particular has stood out in my mind. As I listened, I realized that the voice belonged to someone I knew very well. The individual began by saying; "I'm requesting prayer right at this minute. There is a young lady who had a brain aneurysm some days ago and as we speak, she is having an emergency surgery because she has developed complications." It was a matter of life and death. Immediately I had a flashback. I remembered my sister telling me that on the Tuesday following my surgery, they thought they were going to lose me. I had developed complications—pneumonia.

My sister said she and my mother, on hearing of this new development, began praying and quoting passages from the Psalms. It was a life-and-death situation. Shortly after the doctors returned to my room and informed my mother and sister that the pneumonia had cleared up and there was no need for them to insert a trachea in my throat. God heard desperation in the prayers offered on my behalf by my mother and sister. He immediately answered.

This reminded me of this promise in the Bible, "It shall come to pass, That before they call, I will answer; And while they are still speaking, I will hear" (Isa. 65:24, NKJV). At that moment, I was connecting with this young lady. I closed mine eyes and prayed along with the female presenter on the screen, who had invited the viewers to join her in prayer.

I never found out if the young lady had survived her ordeal, BUT God. I knew that night as I watched that episode of *Let's Pray* that God was very much involved with my case. I needed no evidence or argument to convince me that God loved me. I knew He loved all of us, but like George Matheson, a Scottish minister who became blind at a very young age, I too could also say, "O love that will not let me go," and I found comfort in Deut. 31: 8, NKJV: "And the Lord, He is the One who goes before you. He will not leave you nor forsake you; do not fear nor be dismayed."

"I have been young, and now am old; Yet I have not seen the righteous forsaken, Nor his descendants begging bread" (Ps. 37:25, NKJV).

Chapter 7

The Brook Began to Dry Up

The moment I fell ill, my husband sprang into action. He immediately contacted the principal of the school at which I worked at the time and informed her of my sudden illness. She was very instrumental in assisting my husband with applying for my Family Medical Leave (FMLA). Having waiting for a month, without getting a response to my application, I decided to call the Human Resources section of the Education Department. And it was then that I found out that my leave application was never signed by the superintendent of the School District. The papers were sitting on someone's desk. I completed the call, and next got in touch with the school secretary. I told her what I'd just learned. So, between the school, the District Office, and the Human Resources Office of the Department of Education, the matter was soon to be resolved. But not so fast! I had some more waiting to do.

Sitting up was still a challenge for me. However, there were other application forms pertaining to my sabbatical leave that I was able to complete and have signed by the neurologist whose care I was under at the time. Next, my husband took the completed forms to my principal. I thought I had reached the end of the tunnel. But to my surprise, the process came to a sudden stop again! I felt that I was back to square one. It took a while for it to be resolved. During the process my principal continued to show interest in my case.

One day while I was still in rehab, Wendell made a call to the union office. On the other end of the line he heard a voice. After telling the woman what he was about, she proceeded to outline the steps he should take to get the help I needed.

After proceeding with the given steps, still there was no movement with my case. The volunteer my husband had previously met over the phone while I was in rehab eventually became my passport in moving my case from one place to the next. By this time I was no longer in rehab, and although I was still unable to move independently, while lying in bed I'd be in contact with her at least once a week. She was very professional and knowledgeable. When she spoke, I could hear compassion and kindness. I cannot recall her being harsh and unkind. She was always quick to help. We've never met her in person, but we believe she was God sent. (I often referred to as one of my angels).

The principal I worked with had now retired; however, there was still a letter that needed to be signed by the new principal and submitted to the Department of Education before my case could have moved further. My "angel" asked me if I had gotten the letter signed. My response to her was in the negative. Then she said to me, "someone is standing by my desk, and I'd like you to speak with him." The voice switched to that of a male, and I gave him the history regarding my case. After I was through telling my story, he told me to immediately send him an email, authorizing him to act on my behalf. The authorization letter would give him permission to get the letter signed by the new principal and file a grievance regarding the issues I was having with my salary. Problem solved! Authorization letter was eventually signed by the new principal and returned to the Union office.

As soon as I was through with the telephone call, I got my walker and slowly went over to the computer. I remember the first time I tried using the computer. First, it looked like a foreign object. It was as if I was seeing a computer for the first time. I couldn't figure out how to turn the computer on. It also took me some time to re-familiarize myself with the keyboard. With continuous practice, I eventually was able to use the computer again.

It was now January 2012, and there was still no light at the end of the tunnel. I couldn't travel around as I used to in order to get things done. I was getting nowhere on the phone; neither was there any sign of relief. I wasn't hearing from the Human Resources Section at the head office, the District Office, Union, or the school. At the time, I worked at a school in New York, but due to distance, I was unable to go into Manhattan to find out what was going on with my case.

At the end of June 2012 (the end of the school year), I received a letter from the school where I'd worked. I immediately tore the envelope and enclosed inside was a check with the words *supplemental check* written on the pay advice portion. To me, the word supplemental meant "in addition to." In the first place, to date I'd yet to receive a payment. So, I decided I wouldn't cash the check because I didn't know what the check was for. I also found it very strange that I'd received a paper check when I always got paid through direct deposit.

For seven months, I didn't receive any money. School was now out on summer break, so there was no one at the school or the District Office I could call to find out what the check was for. So, I ended up calling the Human Resources section at the Education Department and each time I'd called I was either transferred from one individual to the next or placed on long holds until I got frustrated and hung up the phone. I got nowhere. It was after making the final call that I decided to keep the check. I needed more information.

However, God kept providing anyway. I had to believe Him when He said in His Word: "Therefore I say unto you, Take no thought for your life, what ye shall eat, or what ye shall drink nor yet for your body, what ye shall put on" (Matt. 6:25, KJV). After a few weeks, the wait was over. This was it, I had no more stumbling blocks in the way. From then on everything was going to be fine, or so I'd thought.

Until one day, after still waiting again for several weeks, I decided to call the Payroll Department. On the other end of the line was a male voice. After a warm hello, I told him what I was calling about. Next, he requested my file number. I gave him the number, and he said he was going to look at my salary history. To my amazement, the man told me that checks were made out in my name and were sent to me.

I told him that I'd never received any remunerations since I'd been out sick, and what he was saying was news to me. I told him that the only check I'd received was a supplemental check, which I never cashed because in the first place, I didn't understand why it was sent to me. He proceeded to tell me that it was my responsibility to find out where the checks were and no action would be taken until I could account for the checks. I told him that I wouldn't be able to find out what had happened to the checks because I was home in my bed, unable to walk.

I didn't prolong the conversation. I told him thanks, ended the call, and tried to make sense of what I'd just heard. I felt very discouraged, but I was able to put the missing pieces of the puzzle together. The supplemental check was issued to me in addition to the checks they thought I'd gotten from November 2011 to May 2012. After regaining my composure, I called the school secretary and informed her about the previous telephone call I'd made, what I'd learned from the call, and what had to be done regarding the checks that were issued in my name before my case would be given further consideration.

The secretary then told me that before I called, she'd received a call from a man, asking her about the checks. He told her that he was requesting that all the checks that were issued in my name be returned to the Payroll Section. That was the last I'd heard about the missing checks. The "supplemental" check was still in my possession. After some weeks had passed, I received a telephone call from the school secretary requesting that I returned the supplemental check to her. Which I gladly did.

By this time, my leave time with pay was coming to an end. I had only two options: to apply for leave without pay or retiring. These were two decisions I found difficult to make. My illness was viewed as catastrophic; therefore, recovery was taking much longer than I'd thought. How would we approach this decision? What steps should we take? Yes, my husband and I prayed and discussed the matter. Reaching a final decision was not an easy one. We both knew that we had to rely on God's leading. We had read many times over in the Bible to "Trust in the Lord with all thine heart; and lean not unto thine own understanding. In all thy ways acknowledge him, and he shall direct thy paths" (Prov. 3:5, 6, KJV). My career was on the line here.

I couldn't rely on my optics, neither my emotions. This time I had to really trust God! We knew that the Word of God stated that "a man's heart plans his way, But the Lord directs his steps" (Prov. 16:9, NKJV). I was caught between a rock and a hard place. On my side, no money was coming in to meet our expenses. We existed for approximately a year on one salary—that of my husband.

The storm clouds had gathered. I looked to the east, then to the west, to the north, and to the south. It looked like a starless night. All around me was total chaos and darkness. However, I knew that our sovereign God was not a God of chaos but a God of order. It was emotionally draining for me, but I had to completely rely on God. There were days when the situation looked very clear to me, and other times when nothing made sense. I began to view my life as one big mess. But never did I asked God "Why?" Because I'd believed if I asked Him for an answer, I would be disappointed with the answer I'd received. Deep in my heart I knew that not one of God's promises would fail me.

So, I decided that I would leave the matter alone and let God be God! Sometimes praying became a challenge. While other times it was just a natural thing to do. On my faith journey with God, I tried taking Him at His Word. I believed that what He said, He'd do. I read Numbers 23:19 that said; "God is not a man that he should lie," and I couldn't recall a time when I'd robbed God of His tithes and offerings.

I'd experienced first-hand Mal. 3:10–11 (KJV) where God stated:

> Bring ye all the tithes into the storehouse, that there may be meat in mine house, and prove me now herewith, saith the Lord of hosts, if I will not open you the windows of heaven, and pour you out a blessing, that there shall not be room to receive it. And I will rebuke the devourer for your sakes, and he shall not destroy the fruits of your ground, neither shall your vine cast her fruit before the time in the field, saith the Lord of Hosts.

I believed that this promise still held true, and I was counting on God to come through for me again one more time!

As a follower of Christ, I knew I wasn't immune from sickness, disease, disappointment, setbacks, and pain. As long as I lived on a planet called Earth, I'd be caught in the middle of the great controversy between Christ and Satan. However, the choice was mine to be on the side of Christ or the other side. I couldn't recall cheating God of what rightfully belonged to Him. I did what was expected of me, and instead I was feeling robbed and cheated. How could God, the God I loved, allow this to happen? I asked the question "how" but never "why."

By this time I was making tiny steps around the house. I continued to see God's providential care in my life. Despite some disappointments, I still believed in miracles. Surviving a brain aneurysm rupture was a miracle of itself! My ability to walk again was also a miracle in itself. Praise God! One afternoon, I decided to give my "angel" a call at the union office. I updated her as to what was happening. She was taken aback that I was still having an issue with salary.

The story of the character Job in the Bible became so real to me. Here was a man who loved God, abhorred evil, was obedient, and was very wealthy, yet he ended up losing his children, health, and wealth. I was having a Job experience. But despite Job's losses, he never lost his focus, he never lost his faith, and he never lost his hope. Like Job, I purposed in my heart that, "Though he slay me, yet will I trust him: but I will maintain mine own ways before him" (Job 13:15, KJV). "But he knoweth the way that I take: when he hath tried me, I shall come forth as gold" (Job 23:10, KJV).

I took the story of Job off the pages of the Bible and made it mine. I internalized it so that it became authentic to me. I was living it! I looked for God in my circumstance. I looked for God around me and found Him in the Bible, through prayer, by reading devotional commentaries, spiritual articles, religious books, songs, and journaling. "And ye shall seek me, and find me, when ye shall search for me with all your heart" (Jer. 29:13, KJV).

It wasn't easy doing so! There were days when trusting God proved challenging. I couldn't rely on yesterday's experience to get me through the next day. Each morning was a new beginning for me. Every day, I experienced, psychological, physical, and social turmoil, but the Bible proved its relevance each time I became discouraged.

Again, I remembered the psalmist David, who faced many struggles in his life, yet he cried, "I had fainted, unless I had believed to see the goodness of the Lord in the land of the living," (Ps. 27:13, KJV). Despite despair, disappointments, and discouragements (3D's), I too looked around me and saw God's goodness and drew strength and courage in the midst of chaos. I was still on the land of the living. God was still taking care of me! I was never in want, and I noticed when I began shifting focus from myself and began looking on God's amazing creation, and helping others, my spirit would be lifted.

My trust and dependence on God would be renewed. Every day I kept searching the scriptures for promises to help me cope. Faith-talk was the way to go, and it worked! I realized that the only way I could make it, was to spend quality time with God, being consistent in prayer and reading the Word of God. The Holy Spirit played a huge role in my day-to-day existence.

As the delays continued, my financial responsibilities ballooned! My medical bills were piling up! There were physicians, medical specialists, therapists, and medical laboratories to be paid. Out of frustration, I placed a call to the Human Recourses section but got no answer. I put the phone back in its cradle and, like a wounded animal, wondered what would be my next move.

This was a trying time for me. I was feeling emotionally drained, physically exhausted, and mentally defeated. I felt hard pressed on every side. Nothing, absolutely nothing, was working in my favor. BUT God! Through this ordeal I kept remembering the many narratives and promises in the Bible, and if God had kept me so far, He wasn't going to leave me in the middle of this journey. I only had to trust Him! I knew I was not the only one who had experienced despair, disappointment, and discouragement before. I saw that however there was a thin line that separated them from depression.

I was feeling like David—"Why art thou cast down, O my soul? And why art thou disquieted within me? Hope thou in God: for I shall yet praise him, who is the health of my countenance, and my God" (Ps. 42:11, KJV). I took comfort in knowing that. And I was also buoyed up when I was reminded by the apostle Paul: "We are troubled on every side, yet not distressed; we are perplexed, but not in despair; persecuted, but not forsaken; cast down, but not destroyed (2 Cor. 4:8–9, KJV)." I gained a whole lot of courage to press on!

The same apostle also reminded me of the many hardships he endured: "Thrice was I beaten with rods, once was I stoned, thrice I suffered shipwreck, a night and a day I have been in the deep" (2 Cor. 11:25, KJV). That was some hardship! But in the end, all that hardship was worth it for Paul. And I too, like Paul, had to endure hardship. I'd my own story to tell. I'd to be an overcomer.

"I sought the Lord, and he heard me and delivered me from all my fears" (Ps. 34:4, NKJV).

Chapter 8

Unexpected Changes

In the meantime, I felt like I was drowning in my tears. It was as if I was surrounded by the enemy of circumstance. It just got bleaker and bleaker every day. My finance was near depletion, and the time allowed for recuperation was diminishing by the day. I had thought my illness would have lasted for two weeks, only to face the reality as the days turned into weeks, that what I thought was going to be a few days turned out to be months into years. It was as if I was in a dream. This was no joke. Everything at the time looked dismal. My mind kept going back to the story of Job, I felt like I was Job.

Job, the Bible character, had lost all that he had: his wealth, servants, and his children, not to mention the support from his wife and friends. Job was an upright man. His ways pleased the Lord and he was a friend of God. However, how could the God Job loved allowed him to go through such turmoil? In Job 1:20 (KJV), I was reminded that Job, after his losses, tore his clothes, shaved his head, fell to the ground, and worshiped God.

Just reflecting on Job's story, I realized that he was facing a test, the biggest faith test of his life. It was then and there that I found myself doing a text-to-self comparison with the character Job. I too had suffered hardships, and like Job, I had to learn how to worship and trust God despite my major losses just like Job did. When I praised God, I felt relieved. He was the Source of my strength.

As Job declared "Naked came I out of my mother's womb and naked shall I return hither, the Lord gave, and the Lord has taken away; Blessed be the name of the Lord" (Job 1:21, NKJV). It was very difficult for me to accept what I'd read, but as time passed, I slowly and painfully learned to accept the situation for what it was. I resorted to praying more. Pray! Pray! Pray! And trusting God day by day. I knew that He would one day get me through my emotional and physical pain, although at the time I didn't see any light at the end of the tunnel. The end of Job's life story told me so. His end was better than how he began. That was good news for me, not materially but more so spiritually. Alleluia!

I watched as my health, my income, my career further declined. And some friendships slowly slipped away. But with God's help, I stayed the course. I knew deep down in my heart that the God I served would not have brought me so far to let me go.

"Behold, I will do a new thing, Now it shall spring forth; Shall you not know it? I will even make a road in the wilderness. And rivers in the desert" (Isa. 43:19, NKJV).

Each day, I took baby steps, graduating to toddler steps. The right side of my skull and face, in particular my forehead, felt like a piece of cardboard, lifeless and hard to the touch. There were many times when I couldn't identify where an itch was on my scalp. I'd to use a small comb and run it through my hair from the base of my head. Doing so was like sending sensors to the area that was itching. At other times I was unable to identify the itch and would gently pat the base of my head next to my right ear to get relief. Relief would come approximately after five or six strokes relief would eventually come.

The skin over my right eye looked like a snake shedding its skin. The sensation on the left side of my face was different from that on the right side. The brain aneurysm had affected all my modalities. Now my taste buds were all on the opposite side, what should have been sweet was now sour, and vice versa. When I ate, the upper right quadrant of my mouth including the right side of my tongue blew up like a balloon. And it would take at least half an hour for that side of my mouth to return to its normal shape.

Whenever I ate or drank, the contents of my mouth would escape from the lower right corner. Chewing food was an uphill task for me. I was only able to chew on the left side of my mouth. Now instead of eating with a fork I was now eating with a spoon. It would seem that my tongue would embark on a salt hunt from the foods I ate. Whether foods were cooked or uncooked my tongue would go in search for the salt. Eating was not an enjoyable experience any more. However, despite the discomfort, I had to eat to survive.

After seven years, my mouth was in so much distress that I had to undergo four oral surgeries. My teeth and gums on both side of my mouth, in particular the upper portions, had to be completely repaired. Bleeding was the order of the day. Coupled with that, when my tongue made contact with the roof of my mouth, next to the upper right molars, it felt like a small, hard pimple had begun to grow there. This gave me cause for concern. So, it was recommended that I saw a dental specialist for professional advice and evaluation. After taking a batch of oral X-rays, undergoing an oral examination, and taking photos of the area, it was determined that it was just a bone growing down from the roof of my mouth. And there was no cause for concern. However, I was advised that if the shape and size changed, I should return.

At the onset of the brain aneurysm, my mouth had shifted from its original position. And every night before retiring to bed, my caregivers would use a mixture of essential oils to massage the right side of my face. The consistent nightly massages eventually paid off. Gradually my mouth returned to its rightful place.

My lips felt like an invasion of ants marching from left to right. And felt like they were constantly on fire. This feeling eventually engulfed the right side of my face pulling on my right eye. I call this "my private hell". I refer to this experience as my "private hell" because someone would be looking directly on my face without knowing or having a clue what was going on. The only time I didn't have that sensation was when I am asleep. The minute I woke, I had to face my "private hell" all over again. This continued for nine years and counting. I knew that the only way I could have kept my sanity was to stand on God's promises. "When you pass through the waters, I will be with you; And through the rivers, they shall not overflow you. When you walk through the fire, you shall not be burned, Nor shall the flames scorch you. For I am the Lord your God" (Isa. 43:2–3, NKJV).

Shortly after returning home from rehab, I began having issues with both elbows. I had difficulty resting both on any given surface. I experienced tingling and numbness that were so unbearable, I had to wear elbow pads for some time. The tingling and numbness extended to the fingers on my left hand and toes. I remember one morning when I opened my eyes a terrible feeling took over my body. The tingling and numbness in my fingers and toes was so severe that I began to feel nauseous. It was then that my husband made the decision to call an ambulance. I was lifted from my bed, placed on a stretcher and into the ambulance, where I was closely monitored by two EMT technicians.

All this time, my husband along with both my parents drove behind the ambulance as it transported me to the emergency room. On reaching the emergency room, I was evaluated, and ended up doing a MRI of my brain. The doctors decided then that I should be kept for a while for further observation. They were unable to find the cause of the tingling, numbness, and nausea. However, they recommended to my husband that I should be seen by a cardiologist.

On my first visit to the office of the cardiologist, I was put on an exercise bike, and my heart rate was monitored to see how I reacted to stress. The following Tuesday, I returned to the cardiologist office where I was subjected to an EKG. This time, my carotid arteries were checked to see if they were clear, and the supply of blood to my brain, neck and face was normal. The results of both tests were negative. Every two years I've had to undergo an MRI to monitor brain activity.

Despite the fear that gripped me, I remembered "In quietness and confidence shall be your strength" (Isa. 30:15, KJV). I had read this promise several years back in the Bible and now the time had come for me to claim it. From this promise I was reminded that there was no need for me to worry; all was required of me was to stay calm and trust God to work the situation out. God was able to make what seemed terribly wrong become right. There was no need to fear. "Whenever I am afraid, I will trust you," (Ps. 56:3, NKJV).

"You-Are-the-God-Who-Sees; for she said, Have I also here seen Him who sees me?"
(Gen. 16:13, NKJV).

Down-and-Out

At this time, I felt as if my whole world was collapsing. I felt trapped in my circumstance. God had to do something! Time was against me. Something had to be done. The story of Hagar, Sarah's Egyptian servant and Abram's wife came to mind (Gen. 16: 1–16; 21:8–21, KJV). I recalled Hagar's wilderness experience and equated it with mine. Sara who was childless had given her servant Hagar to Abraham as wife so that Abraham would have an heir.

Hagar eventually got pregnant and began to brag on Sara, her mistress. This became too much for Sara to handle, resulting in her complaining to Abraham and mistreating Hagar. The conflict between the two women led to Hagar eventually running away. But God had seen Hagar's plight and sent an angel to minister to her. I knew that God was seeing my plight also. Nothing was making sense! For the second time I called the Human Recourses Department to inquire about my Family and Medical Leave Act (FMLA) application.

On the other end of the telephone line I was told by a lady that they had never received my Family and Medical Leave Act (FMLA) application papers. When at the same time while talking with her, I was holding a copy of the submitted application in my hand, with the stamp showing the date, time of delivery, and signature of the person who received the papers in the office. It was then that the conversation took a turn for the good.

All along I felt like Hagar, the handmaiden of Sarah. Through no fault of hers, she was mistreated, and abused by her mistress. She then fled to the wilderness, pregnant and hopeless until one day God showed up. He called Hagar by her name. He knew exactly what had happened to her and saw her predicament. I too was overwhelmed with the circumstances surrounding me, and like Hagar, felt discouraged and hopeless; I also needed direction. Although He knew, the Angel of the Lord asked Hagar where she came from and where she was heading. Hagar told her story. The Angel of the Lord told her what she should do next. First, He told her to return home.

Next, He made her aware that the child she was carrying would one day become the father of a large nation and his name was to be Ishmael, because the Lord had heard her affliction. No longer was Hagar sad and hopeless. There was hope for her and her child. She was overjoyed that God had spoken to her. All wasn't lost for Hagar! And all wasn't lost for me too! I took solace in Hager's story, and my faith was renewed. Hope was still alive!

"But she said to them, Do not call me Naomi; call me Mara, for the Almighty has dealt very bitterly with me" (Ruth 1:20, NKJV).

I continued making text-to-self connections with Bible characters. This was another outlet for me to deal with my emotional, physical, and spiritual pain. I saw myself in another Bible character, Naomi. There were days when I found myself wearing Naomi's shoes. Here was a woman who started off well. She left her homeland married with two sons, but due to a famine, she had to go to Moab where there was food. After settling down in Moab, her husband and two sons died. Life for her became extremely difficult. There was nothing left for her in her adopted homeland but two daughters-in-law. All that she experienced was disappointment, hopelessness, suffering, pain, and bitterness.

After the death of her husband and two sons, Naomi eventually made the choice to return to her homeland with her daughter-in-law, Ruth, volunteering to go with her, where food was now in abundance. On returning home, she was greeted by the women of her town as Naomi. The women were very happy to see her. However, her heart was bathed with pain, sorrow, and bitterness because of what she'd experienced in Moab. Due to her bitter experiences, she told them she no longer wanted to be called Naomi but Mara because God had dealt bitterly with her. I immediately connected with Naomi. By the end of her story, she was restored by God. He provided for her in ways she'd never had expected. His love and concern for her was evident right through the narrative but she was so focused on her trials that she was missing out on God's faithfulness to her. Her end was better than her beginning!

Joy returned to Naomi again. In this narrative I learned that God, whose ways are past finding out, worked out everything for Naomi's good. As Jeremiah wrote "For I know the thoughts that I think toward you, says the Lord, thoughts of peace and not of evil, to give you a future and a hope" (Jer. 29:11, NKJV). So I decided to take an inventory of my life. The first question I asked myself, was this punishment for something I'd done that I was not aware of? Was this payback time? Was I an unfaithful and disobedient steward regarding my time, temple, treasure, and talent? However, one question I didn't asked God was—Why? I didn't want to get to the place of bitterness and harbor resentment. Instead, I yearned for "and the peace of God, which surpasses all understanding" (Phil. 4:7, (NKJV). And just like Paul, I wanted to learn "to be content in the state I had found myself."

At first being at peace with myself was very challenging because I found it very difficult to accept the situation I was facing. And how much time and money I had expended to be at the place I was then. It began some years before in my native Jamaica and accelerated when I immigrated to the United States. I left Jamaica as a trained early childhood education teacher with several years of teaching experience.

On immigrating to New York in the early part of the eighties, I decided to further my education in one of its colleges. I wanted to continue in early childhood education, but God had another plan. Instead of early childhood education, I pursued a Bachelor of Science degree in Special Education. To this day, I cannot tell how I ended up pursuing a first degree specializing in Special Education.

At the time I wasn't employed as a teacher yet, but I had a full time job and attended college after work in the evenings. I did this for four years, Spring, Summer, Fall, and Winter whether rain, or shine. After four years of study, I graduated with a Bachelor of Science Degree in Education with honors, and the year I graduated, I received the college's award for the student who impacted the lives of underprivileged children.

I just didn't stop there; I decided to continue my education, and went on to pursue the Masters of Science in Special Education, with the main concentration in learning disability. I'd no idea that I was going to pursue such a field. It was pure divine intervention that I

Unexpected Changes

found myself focusing on learning disabilities. This was a blessing in disguise. I really enjoyed my course of study.

After my second year, I decided to sit for the New York Teacher's License examination while pursuing the master's degree program and working a full-time job. God was so good to me that I passed the exam on my first sitting.

Looking back, I could see God actively at work, opening doors, for me to walk through that I never dreamed of or saw coming. One of those doors was, I had the opportunity to be a guest lecturer at a prestigious college in New York City. After completion of my master's degree, I continued at the job I was doing. Then after a few months, I began to work at a public school in New York City. I really loved working with my colleagues, students, parents and as liaison for special education for the school where I worked.

But my world changed on the morning of October 8, 2011. I could only equate the upheaval and disturbance in my life to a tsunami. Everything that I'd labored for and invested time and money in went up in smoke. What could I do? I had to make a choice. Do I continue to trust Sovereign God, or do I give up my faith in Him? I chose the former. I decided that in order to get through this turbulent period in my life, I'd to lean on God.

Now my relationship with God was under fire. Was my faith theoretical or experiential? Now the rubber was meeting the road. I'd to constantly keep in mind the sovereignty of God and believed that He would show up in ways I'd never expected. I felt like I left my island home full, and now I had come up empty. I'd lost everything. How much worse could it have gotten? But there was more to come.

"I thank my God upon every remembrance of you"
(Phil. 1:3, NKJV).

Chapter 9

ATTITUDE OF GRATITUDE, THANKS, AND PRAISE

Approximately three years had passed, and I wanted to show thanks to all who were a part of my journey. I wanted to meet the doctors, nurses, and others who had played a role in my surgery and rehabilitation. I just wanted to let each person know how much I appreciated them and the supportive role they played in my recovery. So, I asked my sister who made handmade cards to help me convey thanks to all these people. Without hesitation, my sister got to work and made several cards. No two cards were alike. Each card had a personal touch and expressed a message of thanks.

Now, the question was, how'd I reach these people, in particular, the doctors and nurses? This question was quickly answered by Alberto. I got the cards together, and one morning, Alberto came to my home and drove me to the hospital. I was no longer able to walk without support. I'd to rely on a cane as my assistive device, due to my ongoing mobility issues. On reaching the hospital, I slowly got out of the car and with the aid of my cane, cautiously made my way to meet the male nurse who was very attentive to me while I was in the ICU, whom my sister had told me about. I really wanted to meet him.

So, my first stop was at the ICU nurses' station. It was a long walk for me, and although I felt fatigued, I still sauntered on until I finally reached my destination. On reaching the nurses' station, I gave the nurse sitting at the desk the name of the nurse I'd come to see. She called his name over the intercom, and there he appeared. I introduced myself and immediately he remembered my case. I thanked him verbally and handed him the card that was specifically handmade for him. I bid him goodbye and then began my journey down the long corridor to my other destination.

My next stop was the surgeon's office. I took my time and entered his office. We greeted each other, he asked me how I was doing, and I handed him the card and verbally thanked him for what he had done for me. He was taken aback that a patient had returned to express thanks to him for playing a crucial part in their survival. There was nothing more to be said. So, I turned and left his office.

My final stop was the X-ray department. When I got there, I was told that I had just missed the doctor. So, I left the card with his secretary and slowly made my way, with assistance, to the car.

At home, I continued focusing on getting the rest of the handmade personalized cards to others who had supported me in one way or the other. In Luke, chapter 17 (KJV), the story is told of ten lepers. These were men who had a debilitating disease. They wanted to be healed, and they reached out to Jesus. He heard their cries and gave them instructions: "Go show thyself to the priest" (vs. 14.) While on their way to the priest, the men were healed, but only one came back—the Samaritan—to register his thanks to Jesus. The Samaritan who returned didn't express his thanks privately but showed it in a public way: "and one of them when he saw that he was healed, returned and with a loud voice glorified God and fell down on his face at his feet, giving him thanks" (vs. 15).

Like the Samaritan leper, Jesus had done the same for me. I wasn't only praising and thanking Him, but I'd to express my appreciation publicly to all who played a role in my treatment and recovery. My recovery was a miracle full of love and grace. God's name had to be glorified. His love, and faithfulness had to be witnessed by all. My praise, thanks, and gratitude will always go to Him.

Death was at the door, waiting for me, but Jesus sent life to take its place, and today I am alive to tell the story. One of the keys to my remarkable recovery is based upon a thankful heart. Counting my blessings have been very therapeutic for me. God showed up in my life several times in miraculous ways. Each morning when I opened my eyes I was so appreciative of being alive. I'd take the time each day to reflect on God's goodness and where I was coming from to where I was and envisioned where I wanted to be in the years ahead. Without a doubt, I knew that God was going to finish what He'd started.

God's promises are sure and He never goes back on His Word. I'd lost so much, but God had reassured me in His Word:

> So I will restore to you the years that the swarming locust has eaten, the crawling locust, the consuming locust, and the chewing locusts, my great army which I sent among you. You shall eat in plenty and be satisfied, and praise the name of the Lord your God, Who has dealt wondrously with you; and my people shall never be put to shame. (Joel 2:25–26, NKJV)

And I say hallelujah to that!

Praising God also played an integral part in my life. I realized that when I praised God for who He was and what He was doing, I didn't become anxious, fearful, disappointed, discouraged or experienced despair. I admit there were days when everything just seemed bad, days when the sun didn't seemed to shine, and it appeared to be dark and gloomy. So, in order to lift my spirit, I depended on prayer, various genres of music—hymns and contemporary praise music—the scriptures, and the many encouraging telephone calls and get well cards I received.

When I praised God, I shifted the focus off myself and instead looked to Him. Then and only then my Spirit was renewed.

"Greater love has no one than this, than to lay down one's life for his friends" (John 15:13, NKJV).

Family, Friends, and Strangers

While I was hospitalized, in rehab and during my healing process, my biological family was extremely supportive. It began with my husband Wendell and my parents, Iris and Louis. My sister, Maxine, her husband Benedict and sons Geordan and Nicholas never let up. My other siblings: Lloyd, Verne; Mark, Margaret; Verton, Christine; and Donna, and all their children, including Stephanie and her family were also there for me, lending their emotional and physical support.

From the day I became ill, my family members in New York by marriage were all on board. Taking the lead was my sister-in-law Marva, her husband Calvin and her two daughters. Due to my coordination deficits and issues with my fine motor skills that affected my ability to write, including my inability to move, Samantha and Francine became my scribes when needed. And were also part of my transportation network.

My husband's other siblings who lived in Jamaica, Cadien his sister, her husband Michael, son Gareth and brother Vermont, his wife Kareen and their children Kathy-Ann, Kurt, and Kelsie visited and were always in touch and in constant prayer on my behalf. In the summer of 2012, Cadien, and her family vacationed with us. Since the brain aneurysm, it was the first time I was venturing with her and her son to a supermarket. It felt very strange. It was as if I hadn't gone into a store before. I held on tightly to the bar on the shopping cart and slowly, and timidly pushed it as I walked around the store.

Pushing the cart taught me something. It was then that I discovered that I could use the cart as an assistive device. It would help me increase my pace when walking. The only problem was, I had difficulty focusing when transitioning from indoors to outdoors and vice versa. Soon, the cart became one of my most effective assistive devices.

God had placed me in a loving and supportive family. I thanked God and still do for the spiritual, physical, and emotional support I'd received from them, whether it was biological or by marriage during this critical season of my life.

After leaving rehab, I needed transportation, and did I get it! Brothers Alberto and Higgins along with others. Elder Benjamin and his wife Karlene and her mother, Lorice, were very supportive. Their daughters, Ashley and Amoy, volunteered their time and used their vehicles to transport me to my medical appointments including personal shopping. I was shown generosity in many varied ways.

During my hospitalization and rehabilitation, I was visited by present and former Pastors their wives and Elders of my church. After returning home, I continued to receive visits and calls from them. Every month religiously, I was supplied with liquid meals by Sister Merna and her family. There were "church mothers" who made goodies, packed in small or large gift bags and sent them to me. Several women, Sisters Blossom, Delphene, Jean R., Joy Mc., June, Lurline, Primrose, Maz M., Sandra B., Thelma M., and Alexandria P. (now deceased), along with many others, who showed their kindness in various ways.

Sister Muriel knitted a beautiful thro for me that reminded me of Joseph's coat of many colors. And she along with Sister Pauline K. from time to time would send me baked goodies. From the inception of my illness Sister Pearl M. would also go shopping for me. She would constantly call and frequently sent tokens expressing her love. She was with me on good days and bad days, giving me encouragement and moral support. Sisters Alice D., and Daisy S. willingly made themselves available to take me to my medical appointments.

There was a time when my mother had to fulfill a doctor's appointment and I couldn't go due to my illness and my husband's work schedule prevented him going with her. It was Brother Willy, a member of my Sabbath School class, number six, that took my mother to the doctor and back home. Class six made up of both male and female were very supportive with their prayers and kind deeds. Sisters Freda, Jennifer, Rose, Floreth and Merril, taking the lead.

In the early part of my illness, when I was home from rehab, my parents were my day caregivers, then one day out of the clear blue my father suddenly fell ill and became unresponsive. At the time my husband was at work. I didn't know what to do. I wasn't in any shape or form to take him to the hospital. So I called Sister Grace, a member of the community of faith, and without hesitation she came to my rescue.

She quickly went into action and assisted my mother in dealing with the situation at hand. I called 911, and an ambulance came. My father was still unresponsive when he was taken to the hospital. Sister Grace went with my mother to the hospital and stayed with her until my brother, Mark went and met her at the hospital.

One morning, after Wendell had already gone to work, and I was home alone, I began feeling nauseous. It strongly reminded me of the day I fell ill. So, I reached for the telephone and called Alberto, also a brother of my faith. He immediately drove over to my home.

After I called brother Alberto, I decided to reach out to brother Errol, a registered nurse and also a brother of the faith, who lived in another county for assistance. I told him what was happening and he told us to leave immediately and meet him at the emergency room. On arriving at the ER, brother Errol was waiting for us. My husband was then called and informed of what was happening. No time wasted, I was admitted and placed under observation. For the entire day, brothers Errol and Alberto both remained with me until my husband arrived later in the evening.

My mother was forced to travel back and forth from the United States to Jamaica because of my father's deteriorating health, coupled with my illness. And my husband had to work (the bills had to be paid). So, during that period, I was home alone.

On another occasion I felt nauseous. I'd been told by the neurologist that when feeling nauseous I should seek immediate medical attention. It was during this period of my illness that I paid close attention to my body and adapted the acronym FAST as a guide to help me identify symptoms of a stroke. (First, I took note whether or not my F̲ace was drooping. Second, I observe if there was any weakness in my A̲rms. Next, I took note of changes in my S̲peech and kept in mind that T̲ime was of utmost importance.)

My first reaction was to call the cell number of my sister in Christ, Sister Paulette, a member of class six. At the time, she was out running an errand. However, she told me that she'd be home in the next half hour. On ending the call, I reached out to Alberto who without hesitation, came and got me at my home and headed straight to Sister Paulette's home. From Sister Paulette's home we headed straight to the emergency room.

On arriving at the emergency room, my name was entered into the computer. From there I received prompt attention. Sister Paulette, stayed with me the entire afternoon, until my husband came after work in the evening. He thanked her and told her she could go if she wanted to, but she insisted on staying. We left the ER after eleven o'clock that night. First, we took her home, and then we headed on home. The MRI that was done didn't show a problem, but the tingling, numbness, and nauseous feeling was still cause for concern.

"Sister Eddy" my prayer partner, (now deceased), every morning rain or shine would call. We'd pray together and she'd encourage me especially on days that were very depressing. Sister Zelma, another member of my faith community, consistently provided transportation to physical therapy twice per week. She'd take me and my mom to the sessions and waited patiently in her car for the hour until the session was completed and then took us home.

Approximately, six years before my illness, I attended a mid-day fasting and prayer service at my church. There I met a motherly lady. Right then and there a friendship blossomed and since then this woman of God has been engrafted into my biological family. My term of endearment for Sister Davidson eventually became "Sister D". Time moved on and "Sister D" relocated to Jamaica. It was during this time that my father fell ill and in my mother's absence she became my father's caregiver. In the meantime my mother was my caregiver in the daytime, while my husband worked.

Over and over again, I've thanked God for placing me in a community of believers who showed in many ways how much they loved and cared for me. Many times, I thought of Elijah the prophet in 1 Kings 17, who God took care of him during a famine and a drought in Israel. God himself told Elijah to go to the brook Cherith. First, God told him he should drink from the brook and He would send ravens to feed him. Elijah obeyed and his bread and water was always sure. God was his Provider. Elijah's story resonated with me. Despite my financial famine and drought, my bread and water was also sure. God was also my provided!

In Mark 2, the story is told of a man who was sick, and his friends wanted him to see Jesus. The place was so crowded that they were unable to enter through the door to take their sick friend to see Him. So, they came up with a brilliant idea. They decided to gain entrance through the roof because there was no room. They let the man down on his mat, and then the man found himself directly in the presence of Jesus. These men wanted their friend to be healed by Jesus, so they used an unconventional way to get it done—through the roof. Mission accomplished! The man was forgiven and healed.

Throughout my ordeal, God placed some extraordinary people in my life to help me along the difficult journey. I called them friends. There were from my community of believers and also people belonging to other faiths and individuals that I knew from my childhood. As a child living in Jamaica, I went to high school with Joanna who has remained my friend for all these years. After graduation, we took different paths.

A few years passed, my husband and I migrated to the United States, and years later Joanna immigrated to England with her family. Despite the expanse body of water that separated us, we still remained friends. We spoke frequently on the telephone. My husband called her a few days after my stroke and informed her about my illness. In a few days, my friend arrived at my doorstep. She spent four and half weeks, helping to take care of me.

One day while reading I stumbled on two quotes that I've used to define what I've experienced. "A strong friendship; doesn't always need togetherness, as long as the relationship lives in the heart, true friends will never part." The next quote "Many people will walk in and out of your life, but only true friends will leave footprints in your heart."

After many months the cryptic message finally came full circle. I'll forever be grateful to Dr. Kadine, my friend for entering my life where she provided physical, spiritual, and emotional support at a time when I needed it the most.

After exiting rehabilitation and receiving out-patient physical therapy service, one evening I received a visit from Dr. Kadine. It was on this visit that I accepted her kind offer of working with me in order to regain my strength, mobility, coordination, and balance. God had sent another angel in the form of Dr. Kadine.

She was very soft spoken, kind, and gentle in her demeanor. A good listener, she showed empathy in the way she worked with me.

I knew I was in good hands, and I never feared doing the exercises. It was then that my mother reminded me about the cryptic message in the hospital. There were many memorable moments that I'll always cherish with Dr. Kadine. One of them I can recall clearly as if it were yesterday was when she took me to the kitchen and taught me how to hold a knife and peel a potato. I wouldn't have imagined that I'd forgotten how to do something as simple as that. It felt very weird and strange. It took a little while for me to hold both the knife and the potato properly in both hands. However, Dr. Kadine was very patient and kept on encouraging me until I completed the task.

Today, I'm able to walk due to the therapy I received from Dr. Kadien, a trained physical therapist, she was very dedicated and instrumental in getting me on my feet again. As I've said in a previous chapter, the outpatient therapy sessions weren't enough. My physical therapist friend, gave up her time and dedicated two days out of her schedule to help me each week.

This was the answer to God's cryptic message He gave me. I felt very blessed and honored that a young person would shelve their personal time to assist me on my road to recovery. Dr. Kadine's family was very supportive. Her mother, Elder Icene cooked and packaged lasagna dishes and on a Friday her dad, Brother Ronald, would bring the package to my home.

On our first meeting, she did an assessment, and from there she developed a program to address my needs. It wasn't one size fits all. I can recall before engaging in any form of activity that she'd offer up a prayer. And then proceed to address issues relating to physical awareness. There were other times when my friend took me on the road and taught me how to cross at the stoplight within the appropriate time. She made each session fun. One evening she took me in her car, and we went to a park in the neighborhood. There my young friend taught me how to walk on different surfaces. It was in the park that I learned to walk and balance on asphalt, gravel, and grass.

Going up and down a staircase without holding on to the bannister was another scary activity. But with her cheering me on, I eventually overcame and conquered my fear. One of my favorite activity was to relearn balancing and walking in my favorite one-and-a-half-inch kitten heel shoe. On my first try, I was very scared. But as time went on, I grew accustomed to walking in my house in those shoes. Over time the shoe earned the name "favor shoes". Because of my illness, I was still unable to attend church services. And, I must admit that my internal emotional landscape was not prepared to return because I feared reliving what took place that fateful Sabbath morning.

My physical therapist friend had a surprise for me. She arrived at my home on a Thursday afternoon, assisted me to the passenger's seat of her car, and drove me to the church building. We made our way to the main entrance of the sanctuary. The doors were already wide open. This was a test of how emotionally sound I was, to go back to the place where it all began.

For a moment, I wept uncontrollably, then I was able to regain my composure, and with my cane, wobbled to the pew where I fell ill. From there, I walked slowly with the aid of my cane up and down the middle aisles and to the altar. I realized that by visiting the scene, I was reconditioning my mind and overcoming the megafear to return. At the end of my visit my fear disappeared, I was an overcomer!

"Nay, in all these things, we are more than conquerors through him that loved us" (Rom. 8:37, KJV). My recliner became very valuable to me. It was a chair where I relearned sitting up on my own and feeding myself with a spoon instead of a fork. One evening, while

Attitude of Gratitude, Thanks, and Praise

eating dinner in that chair, I received a telephone call that would prove to be a game changer.

Eleven years before my illness, on the first day of the new school year, I'd met Kathi, a teacher's assistant. We immediately became friends. During my illness she became very helpful to us. She acted as a liaison between the school and my husband. Whenever there were papers to be handed in to the Principal, she'd arrange with Wendell the day and time they could meet. They'd usually meet very early in the morning on their way to work at the 125th Street subway station in Manhattan.

Unbeknownst to me Friday, October 7, 2011, Columbus Day weekend was going to be my last working day. Everything was left as is. Never in my wildest dreams did I imagine, I wouldn't be returning to the building. Now, I was faced with a dilemma. There were personal belongings that I'd left behind. The question was—how would I get them? I never made any previous arrangements to retrieve them with Kathi. But after I was hospitalized, Wendell called her and informed her that I'd fell ill over the weekend. So on her return to the school building the Tuesday morning, she went into action!

She packed my personal belongings in boxes and arranged with the custodial engineer to put the boxes in storage. Next, she arranged with him to transport the boxes to my home at a later date. To my surprise, one afternoon they both showed up with the boxes at my home. On another occasion, while sitting in my favorite chair, the telephone rang. When I answered, it was the voice of my teacher assistant friend, Kathi.

She wanted to find out how I was doing. We spoke for about fifteen minutes. It wasn't my intent to share with her the issue I was having with my medical coverage. But I told her what was going on anyway. I made known to her that I'd just received the fifth letter from the health division, informing me that my health coverage had been canceled. And I was feeling distressed about it. We spoke for another ten minutes and said goodbye.

The following evening, at approximately five o'clock I received a call. The voice on the other end sounded unfamiliar. I sheepishly said "hello," and then I heard on the other side, "What a friend you have! We saw this lady stepping past us, demanding to see the manager. We eventually got her to slow down and tell us her story. She was furious about the cancellation of your health coverage and was demanding for someone to look into the matter. She said if she had to go to the top to get the matter resolved, she was going to do it." The lady then proceeded to tell me the name of the woman. It was my friend Kathi!

I then asked the lady who I was speaking to at the time to identify herself. She told me that she was the director for the Welfare Services for the Teacher's Union. Then, she requested some pertinent information from me. In twenty minutes, my health coverage was reinstated! It was then that I found out that my papers were mixed up, and miscommunication had also caused the debacle.

Still, unable to visit the various offices to get my papers sorted out, that night I decided that I'd ask Kathi to be my hands and feet. So, between my husband and Kathi, I was able to get my medical paperwork sorted out. Another day I telephoned Kathi and told her that I was going to send her a notarized letter, giving her permission to do business on my behalf. It worked! From then on, the missing parts to the puzzle began filling in.

After the visiting nursing physical therapy service had ended and due to the cancellation of my medical coverage, physical therapy had come to a dead end. One day, out of the clear blue, my husband Wendell, decided to call an 800 number and found himself talking to the director of therapy services at my health insurance provider's office. He told her the history of my story, and that phone call led to many wonderful outcomes. She followed up the telephone conversation by sending a list of physical therapy sites near to my home.

Soon after, I resumed my therapy sessions twice per week. Late one afternoon, I received a call from a lady at the therapy office at the hospital, informing me that my sessions had ended, and I should not report for any more services. The next morning, while lying on my back in my bed, I called the 800 number my husband had previously called and left a voicemail message on the extension. Later that morning, my call was returned. I told my story, and at the end of the conversation, I was told to call the physical therapy department and inform them that I was reporting to my next scheduled appointment in the afternoon.

From then on, more sessions were added. More and more, I saw God's fingerprint all over my life. I saw Him as Jehovah Jireh, my Provider. There were times when a check would unexpectedly arrive in the mail, just in time to take care of an expense. I'd seen Him as my Jehovah Rapha, my Healer. I'd experienced His spiritual, emotional, and physical healing through prayer, through the scriptures, a devotional reading, the words of a song, a motivational quote, the exhorted word in a worship service, or just through nature. What a God!

One evening, I decided to call the retiree at the union office again and in walked into her office the man responsible for grievances. She wasted no time in presenting my case to him. And without hesitation, he immediately got to work. Before the evening was over, emails were leaving my computer to his, and from one office to the next. Within a week, all the roadblocks that took two years to resolve, disappeared! God was on the job!

Fast forward to the year 2018. One morning, I received a call from Sister Sandra Bur. who attended my church. In the conversation, she told me that she'd always wanted to do an act of kindness for me because when her sister was ill some years back, I was there for her. So, she offered to take me to my eye appointments.

After working her night job, this kind lady, would show up at my home on the mornings of my appointments. She would chauffeur me back and forth from my home and, better yet, waited until I saw the doctors. Then she'd go home and rest to go back to her night job. This was where I actually learned the true meaning of the scripture, "Cast your bread upon the waters, For you will find it after many days" (Eccl. 11:1, NKJV).

A few months afterward, God's providence showed up again. A former hairdresser of mine, Yvonne, stopped by my home to see how I was doing and in what ways she could have assisted me. I'd known her for many years. She attended another branch of my church. She introduced me to her friend who had given her the ride to my home. We greeted each other. And it was then that I noticed that his face looked very familiar. I'd seen him somewhere before. It was at my church! That was the beginning of a friendship between Brother Eric and my family—husband, mother, siblings, and nephews.

He has been the go to person for my husband and myself. He'd take me to all my doctor's appointments when my husband was unable to go, due to work and helped us in other situations. We've seen in many, many ways God's hands in our lives. Just when we would hit a roadblock, God would show up. He was always on time sending someone at the right time to rescue us. Over the years, I've grown to trust God more and see His promises fulfilled in my life.

Elder Michelle M, a social worker from my community of believers always availed herself to assist with matters relating to my case. Health care professionals within the community of faith made themselves available also when I needed medical assistance. There were others of the house of faith who volunteered to assist with housekeeping and gave generously. It was really a family affair. I thank God for my church family!

The staff at the rehabilitation center were very kind and considerate. They played a very effective role in my recovery. There was never a time when I felt I was lacking anything. They made sure that I was comfortable and encouraged me when it was time to do the varied exercises. They became a part of the village that was responsible for my recovery.

While in rehab, there were several times loneliness and fear sneaked up on me, and everything around me looked chaotic, I would often take refuge in the promise, "He will not leave you nor forsake you" (Deut. 31:6, NKJV). Jesus became my Jehovah Shalom: "You will keep him in perfect peace, Whose mind is stayed on You, Because he trusts in You" (Isa. 26:3, NKJV).

Whatever I wanted Jesus to be, He became. As time marched on, I accepted my fate, although it was a bitter pill to swallow. With the help of the Holy Spirit, I learned to trust more in Jesus, and to take Him at His word.

"So Philip ran up and heard him reading the prophet Isaiah, and said, 'Do you understand what you are reading?'" (Acts 8:30 NKJV).

Chapter 10

Reading to Understand

As I went to and fro to the various medical appointments which included a heart evaluation and a stress test, I realized that I was still a candidate for depression. So, along with immersing myself in the Bible, praying, listening to uplifting spiritual music and journaling, I went on a quest to find out what had happened regarding my illness. I went in search for books about the brain and aneurysms, the causes and effects, signs, descriptions, treatment, life after a cerebral aneurysm, and ways to heal the brain.

It was my first post-op visit to my neurologist. I was sitting in the waiting room with my friend Alberto, who had taken me there. It was there that he showed me a book titled *Healing the Broken Brain* by Elden M. Chambers PhD. The title of the book really got my attention, so I quickly took it out of his hand, read the blurb, opened it to its first chapter and read until I came to the second chapter, when the following got my attention:

> *Use it or lose it!* ... Of course *disuse,* though possibly the greatest contributor to loss, is not the only contributor ... Destructive foreign substances, insufficient oxygen, incomplete and poor

nutrition, infectious diseases, inappropriate environments, and head injuries also account for much of this loss. Such loss invites the inevitable consequence—*a broken brain!* Incapacitation, spreading degeneration, mental depression, mental confusion, perceptual distortion and a host of emotional disorders! But take heart!" (Elden M. Chambers PhD, *Healing the Broken Brain,* p. 10)

This was the beginning of my search to better understand what the key factors in getting well were. By the help of the Great Physician I purposed in my heart from then on that I was going to do all the right things to get my brain up and running again. Before having audience with the doctor, I gave the book back to my friend. After seeing the doctor, Alberto took me home. I was pleasantly surprised, the next morning, Alberto came to my home and presented me with my own copy of the book he had shown me the day before at the doctor's office. I was so appreciative of his kindness and generosity. He left, and I began where I'd left off reading the day before.

As I read, more and more I realized that the road to recovery was going to be a very long one for me. It was certainly going to be a challenge, but I was reminded by the Holy Spirit "Fear not, for I am with you; Be not dismayed, for I am your God. I will strengthen you, I will uphold you with My righteous right hand" (Isa. 41:10). "Healing the broken brain—overcoming depression, anxiety, panic disorders, etc.—means developing a new set of healing habits" (Elden M. Chalmers PhD, *Healing the Broken Brain,* p.34). When I read this statement, I realized that in order for my brain to be made whole again, I'd have to replace my old habits and ways with new ones.

So I decided to do a complete overhaul of how I handled situations regarding my physical and emotional make-up. I truly had to recalculate and began to develop habits that would prevent me from self-destructing. It never took me long to see that my illness could lead to depression. I'd all the qualifications suited for depression: loss of health, loss of career, and loss of income. There were days when I felt as if I'd failed in all aspects of my life. Moving from all negative thoughts to a positive mind-set proved at first to be very challenging for me. I realized that to begin the process of achieving a healthy mind, I'd to accept the reality of what had occurred and take my mind to a place where I would be at peace with myself. Bitterness, anger and un-forgiveness were negatives, and I was aware that these could stand in the way of my recovery.

The next place I went to find this peace was the Bible "Great peace have they which love thy law; and nothing shall offend them" (Ps. 119:165, KJV).Who could I rely on but the Holy Spirit to help me? I remembered reading somewhere that one way to cultivate positive thinking was to memorize scripture, and this I did. Yes, I'd known some scripture verses before. But this time, I made it a habit to focus and added more scriptures to my repertoire through repetition. As I explored the Bible, I learned so much about God's character. I realized that God loved and cared for me, and He was with me no matter the situation. He wanted what was best for me. Never once did His promises failed!

The more I read, I gradually understood what it would take to make my brain well again. I had to control my thoughts:

> It is most difficult to control your thoughts to imagine positive emotions, or to engage in essential health-producing exercises when in a manic or depressed state, when filled with excessive anxiety, guilt feelings, obsessed with unwanted thoughts or the like ... Use your Brain in healthy ways and

its cells will sprout and multiply new connections for increased productivity and abounding health. Let your brain cells remain *unused* or *abused* and relevant brain cells and their connections will die. (Chalmers, p. 60)

Reading this paragraph, I realized that I had to engage in various mental activities in order to keep my brain cells alive and protect my frontal lobe.

From then on, I began reading books that were spiritually content–based and listened to news that was informational and more on the positive side. My focus was mostly on nonfiction writings, in particular the Bible. I remembered how important critical reading skills were because I once had to teach these skills to children who were struggling readers. When I read, the first thing I focused on was identifying the main idea of a piece. Identifying the main idea was an important reading skill, and I knew that I'd to get back to the place where I was able to do it. So, whenever I read, identifying the main idea of what I was reading was my main objective.

It took some time to relearn the other reading skills, such as prior knowledge, making a prediction, drawing conclusions, sequencing, making inferences, and identifying cause and effect. Each day I worked at one of the skills. The skill of sequencing was the most challenging for me. I've made strides in this area and have continued to work on it. Context is another area that I had to pay close attention to. And so, as I read each day, I tried to identify the context of the pieces I read and of course included the main idea.

My Bible became a source of strength to me. I became fascinated with several of its characters and their relationships with God, especially through times of adversity. I began relying on the many promises in Bible, and made them come alive in my life. To safeguard my mind from straying, I would very often remember the Bible verse: "Finally, brethren, whatsoever things are true, whatsoever things are honest, whatsoever things are just, whatsoever things are pure, whatsoever things are lovely, whatsoever things are of good report; if there be any virtue, and if there be any praise, think on these things" (Phil. 4:8, KJV).

From then my perspective on my circumstance was transformed day by day. Some days anxiety and hopelessness would creep up on me, and I'd be reminded by Holy Spirit not to: "be anxious for nothing, but in everything by prayer and supplication, with thanksgiving, let your requests be made known to God; and the peace of God, which surpasses all understanding, will guard your hearts and minds through Christ Jesus" (Phil. 4:6–7 NKJV). This verse of scripture became another staple from the Bible for me. As days turned into months and months into years, I yearned for the peace that God promised through His Word.

Step by step, the anxiety and hopelessness that tried to cloud my mind began to slowly dissipate. I just kept reading Elder M. Chalmers's book. Two other paragraphs gave me hope. One is found on p. 67: "The brain has the ability to adapt and change ... We need not be permanent victim of our own bad choices and practices." The brain aneurysm was not of my own doing, but it came my way. On the same page, I learned that God had blessed us with two speech (very reassuring to know) areas: the Broca, found in the front part of the brain; and the Wernicke, located in the temporal lobe. It was then that I felt a revival of hope in my heart. With time and practice, I'd be able to talk fluently again!

When one speech area wasn't up and functioning, the other took over. For me, I'd lost my expressive and language skills and my ability to walk and although I'd residual effects in all three areas, through prayer, physical and speech therapies, I was able to talk and walk again. I still don't know the parts of my brain that took over the functions allowing me to talk and walk again. But that's the plasticity of the brain! Our God created us in a magnificent way and the more I read, the Bible verse "I praise you for I am fearfully and wonderfully made; Marvelous are thy works, and my soul knoweth right well" (Ps. 139:14, KJV), the more I understood the text.

I learned also that "The brain plasticity or capacity for compensation and the growth of new connections provide hope for victims of their brain's maladies. Loss of abilities, loss of emotional control, loss of memory, confused thinking, may not have to shape your destiny. The brain's plasticity offers promise for healing" (Chalmers, p. 68). What hope! What joy! All was not lost. It was going to be a challenging journey, but just reading this paragraph gave me peace and hope. Good news! The brain can reshape itself!

I wanted to find out if nutrition played a role in the healing of the brain. One evening while watching *It Is Written*, a Christian program, the discussion title got my attention—"Boosting Your Brain" with John J Bradshaw (host) and Dr. Neil. Nedley (speaker); Bradshaw and Nedley, 2016 *It Is Written Script* 1365 [Boosting Your Brain]. There was a doctor being interviewed by a pastor. The more I listened, the more I realized that nutrition was very important for the brain. The interviewer made reference to God giving us an organ that gave us life–a nerve center called the brain. As I continued to listen, the pastor asked the doctor: what were some things that could improve brain function. The first word that came out of the doctor's mouth was nutrition.

As the interview proceeded, I learned the importance of nutrition to brain health. Having a healthy brain also affects one's relationship with God. In a nutshell, nutrition was all about what we ate. Fat is not good for consumption. There are fats that lead to poor heart function, and if the heart is affected, the brain too would be affected. The doctor proceeded to say that what we ate turned into neurotransmitters which turned into neurons which, in turn, turns into cells responsible to support the function of the brain. A good diet was very important. He further explained what were Omega 3's fats and the role these fats played in having a healthy, functioning brain.

It was the first time I was learning that we human beings and also animals don't have the ability to produce Omega 3 fats. In order to get these essential fats, we had to include these fats in our diet through eating or drinking. Fish was the main source of Omega 3, which I ate every now and then. But when I heard the doctor mentioned whole wheat, wheat germ, walnuts, chia seeds, and good, old flax, I was excited to know that I was on the right path. Every morning my breakfast consisted of a large glass of smoothie containing almond milk, a ripe banana, strawberries, blueberries, and sprinkled on top was a tablespoon of freshly, ground flax. Sometimes, I would alternate between whole fruits and smoothies.

The interviewer asked the good doctor if he could find a character in the Bible whose diet played an important role in his or her life. The answer was the prophet Daniel in Daniel chapter 1. Thoughts were also important. My thoughts could be distorted. I could magnify my thoughts or minimize them, and a Bible character who did this a lot was King Saul.

In another episode Pastor Bradshaw, and Dr. Nedley had a conversation on the topic "Controlling Your Emotions." In this episode, I learned that there were several factors that could lead to mental illness; the biggest factor was the sin of *pride*. This could eventually lead to poor self-esteem, poor self-worth, and a feeling of worthlessness Bradshaw and Nedley, 2015. *It Is Written Script* 1360 [Controlling Your Emotions]. Knowing this was very important to me because I'd lost my health, my career, and my income, which could have led me down the path of depression or thinking suicidal thoughts. Christ was my perfect example, and I'd have to keep my focus on Him in order not to fall into the pit of depression.

As I continued listening to the interview, the doctor spoke about the importance of emotional intelligence and how it affects our thinking. I was very impressed when the doctor used several Bible characters to substantiate his points. We see in some of these characters that several things can lead to depression. I was not alone. God had given His Word for me to see how He deals with us on our own level and how our circumstances can differ. I was reassured when I read this "When you pass through the waters, I will be with you; And through the rivers, they shall not overflow you; When you walk through the fire, you shall not be burned, Nor shall the flame scorch you" (Isa. 43:2 NKJV).

Dr. Nedley made reference to the prophet Elijah who faced a difficult time in his life. He was a righteous man, and yet that difficult time led him into depression. His thoughts became negative and he felt emotionally drained and defeated. No longer was he thinking straight. Elijah had just witnessed God's great power at Mount Carmel. Yet, after Queen Jezebel threatened him, this man of God fled for his life and ended up under a broom tree in the wilderness. There he sat and prayed to God and said, "It is enough! Now, Lord, take my life, for I am no better than my fathers" (1 Kings 19:4 NKJV). Then he fell asleep. There, God sent an angel to wake him up. The angel told him "arise and eat" (1 Kings 19:5 NKJV). Elijah did eat and drink and went back to sleep a second time. But the angel appeared again and encouraged him to eat because he had a long journey ahead of him. So, in order to gain strength to take his journey that would last forty days and forty nights to Mount Horeb, Elijah ate again.

On reaching Mount Horeb, Elijah found refuge in a cave. He was there for a night. The cave and the night were symbols of the dark experience I was enduring at the time. Despite his state of mind, God still took care of him! I took solace in this story because here was a man of God whose faith failed him, and as a child of God, my faith at times failed me also. Like Elijah, my emotional health frayed, but God, in His love and mercy, helped me through this dark stage of my life. I needed to get myself emotionally well again by paying more attention to nutrition, exercise, water, sleep, temperance (self-control), air, rest, and trust in God.

While in the cave, Elijah was visited by God. God asked him what he was doing in the cave and in his depressive emotional state he verbalized to God what he had done on his behalf. God heard him and God acted! Then, God instructed Elijah, "go out, and stand on the mountain before the Lord" (1Kings 19:11 NKJV). Elijah obeyed and then a strong wind blew and the rocks on the mountain moved out of their place and broke apart but God was not in it. Next, it was an earthquake, but God was still not in it. Then came a fire but unlike Moses who saw the bush burning in the wilderness (Exod. 3:1-15 NKJV), a symbol of God's presence, in Elijah's case, God was still not in the fire. Instead God showed up in a still small voice! Like Moses, who removed his sandals from his feet, Elijah wrapped his face with his mantle on hearing the still small voice, as a symbol of God's holiness and presence. On reading the narratives of these two patriarchs, Moses and Elijah, and their experiences with God in the wilderness and on Mount Horeb, I took an inventory of my life and applied the very valuable lessons I learned from them.

Day by day, I realized I'd nothing to fear because God was in control of my life! "For God has not given us a spirit of fear, but of power and of love and of a sound mind" (2 Tim. 1:7, NKJV). All I had to do was to take care of myself, keep my faith in God, trust

Him, and leave the rest to Him. He'd assured me through many Bible promises that He would take care of me. No matter what I was facing, my mantra was trust God!

"Finally, brethren, whatsoever things are true, whatever things are noble, whatever things are just, whatever things are pure, whatever things are lovely, whatever things are of good report, if there is any virtue and if there is anything praiseworthy-meditate on these things" (Phil. 4:8 NKJV).

A Sound Mind

A sound mind! How could I foster a sound mind in the midst of chaos? At the time, through my lens, nothing seemed to be going great in my life. Another book that came to my rescue, was a small publication called *A Sound Mind: Thinking Your Way to Vibrant Health* by Sharon Platt-McDonald. In her book, the author stated that "One of the reasons for negative emotions and negative self-talk is our inability to get over the hurts of the past" (Platt-McDonald, *A Sound Mind,* p. 30). From reading this statement, I knew I'd have to get pass my negative emotions and negative self-talk in order to be made spiritually and physically whole again.

I believed that the Holy Spirit was in tune with my brokenness and saw my eagerness to move on. He saw that I was searching for answers, and the more I searched, the more I found what was needed to make it happen. It was my responsibility, with the help of the Holy Spirit, to filter the thoughts that entered my mind. Who better to turn to for help but Jesus? "Let this mind be in you, which was also in Christ Jesus" (Phil. 2:5, NKJV). From then on, I indulged in positive self-talk and instead of looking at the darkness engulfed me, I tried clinging to Jesus, even through my tears. There were many days when I shed tears and many nights that my pillow was soaked. Because in my eyes, the future wasn't looking good for me.

I'd been through several other health challenges before (fractured my right tibia and the retina detachment in my right eye) but the present proved to be the most challenging of all. This was a life-changing experience for me, and I needed help to cope. I felt at the time I'd lost everything I'd ever dreamed of and worked for. At the time, my faith in God was challenged, but I kept going back to my main point of reference—the Bible. "In the day I cried out,

You answered me, And made me bold with strength in my soul" (Ps. 138:3, NKJV). I had to call on God every single day to face the pain and suffering I was experiencing. Most of the books I read spoke about acceptance, resignation, and moving on when faced with suffering and pain.

Platt-McDonald quoted from Creath Davis that:

> Resignation is surrender to fate. Acceptance is surrender to God. Resignation lies down quietly in an empty universe. Acceptance rises up to meet the God who fills that universe with purpose and destiny. Resignation says "I can't." Acceptance says, "God can." Resignation paralyses the life process. Acceptance releases the process for its greatest creativity. Resignation says "It's all over for me." Acceptance says, "Now that I'm here, what's next Lord?" Resignation says, "What a waste." Acceptance says, "In what redemptive way will You use this mess, Lord?" Resignation says, I'm alone." Acceptance says, I belong to you Lord. (Platt-McDonald, p. 59)

The choice was mine to make, acceptance or resignation. The moment I read the statement above, I chose acceptance. I could view my situation as a lemon and use it to make lemonade or let it remain a lemon.

One morning, some years back when the retina in my right eye detached, and I was getting ready to fulfill my post-op visit to the eye specialist, the Lord showed me in His Word "Behold, I have refined thee, but not with silver, I have chosen thee in the furnace of affliction" (Isa. 48:10 KJV). At the time I was alone in the room and all I could do was to cry aloud, "Lord, if this is how You're going to make me into what You want me to be, You'll have to walk with me through it!" From then on there was a sequence of several health issues. Each one had its own unique feature and showed up unexpectedly. To this point the most serious of them was a near death experience caused by a brain aneurysm that had an impact on my entire brain function and changed my entire life. By God's grace, I wasn't going to allow fate to become ruler over my life. But to use the principles of acceptance, to move on with my life and make something beautiful of it.

I desperately wanted to walk again and go back to business as usual. My cerebellum (the little brain) was severely broken and needed repair. I just couldn't see myself sitting in a wheelchair for the rest of my life and having to deal with a severe speech impediment at the same time. I couldn't depend on the speech sessions I was getting twice per week. I needed much more. One night shortly before retiring to bed, I came across a particular scripture in the Old Testament. I truly believed that the Holy Spirit guided me to that particular book that night. The book was Habakkuk. My eyes froze on the words: "And the Lord answered me, and said, Write the vision, and make it plain upon tables, that he may run that readeth it. For the vision is yet for an appointed time; but at the end it shall speak, and not lie; though it tarry, wait for it; because it will surely come, it will not tarry" (Hab. 2:2,3, KJV). I believed that God was sending a message my way.

After reading this scripture, I was assured that I was going to walk again. It would take some time for my speech to improve, and once again I'd be able to independently take care of myself. No more would I be confined to a wheelchair and unable to independently take care of myself. I just had to be patient and wait on the Lord. It would certainly happen. I'd my goals and objectives regarding where I'd wanted to see myself in six months since I'd left rehab in a wheelchair on the Tuesday before Thanksgiving, 2011. I was resilient and determined by God's grace to get rid of the wheelchair. So on the last Wednesday of February 2012, the wheelchair was no more. I'd moved on to another assistive device—a walker.

Within six months, the walker was gone. I graduated from a wheelchair to a walker, and I continued to work daily on my speech, trusting God and leaning on His many promises. There were good days and not so good days ahead. As the days turned into months, I continued my outpatient hospital occupational and speech therapy sessions, and God provided much more. As a former special education teacher, I decided that I'd incorporate many of the teaching strategies I used with my former students to aid me in my rehabilitation because I'd difficulty with execution, retention and reinforcement.

Working with numbers became a challenge, especially math word problems and telling time. My phonemic awareness skill, my expressive and receptive language skills were all affected due to visual impairment, the loss of hearing in my right ear and speech impediment. However, I was able to carve out for myself daily activities, such as reading daily the Bible, devotionals, religious magazines, books, commentaries written by Christian authors, and journaling. These activities were supplemented by word finds, scriptural crossword puzzles, pictorial puzzles, and watching Christian television networks.

One bright summer evening, I was now using a cane, I bravely went shopping with my husband to a large department store. There, in the store I met a brother in Christ, Walter. I'd not seen him in ages. We exchanged greetings and spoke for a little while. It was during our conversation that he encouraged me to read the book *If You Want to Walk on Water You've Got to Get Out of the Boat* by John Ortberg. On reaching home, I immediately went online and purchased the Kindle version of the book. I read the book from cover to cover and found it very motivational. From then on I became interested in books written by Christian authors.

My second purchase of a book written by Christian authors, was entitled *Joni & Ken An Untold Story* by Ken and Joni Eareckson Tada. I went online and got the Kindle version of the book. It was a text-to-self book for me written by Joni, a disabled woman, paralyzed from her waist down due to a diving accident at the age of seventeen, and her spouse Ken, who married her despite her disability. Ken was not only Joni's husband, but also her primary caregiver. I immersed myself in the book. As I read, I learned how they were able by God's grace to weather the emotional rollercoaster ride in their marriage and to deal with Joni's disabilities.

They wrote about how they'd weather the storms in their marriage and managed to keep the romance alive. Written on each page of the book, was the respect they had for each other. And Jesus was the center of their union. They prayed and read their Bible together and shared Jesus' love with people, young and old, all over the world through various ministries. Joni turned her disabilities into possibilities. Today she's a well-known motivational speaker, author, painter, and have her own disability ministry. She is the founder and CEO of *"Joni and Friends"* International Disability Center. Ken, her husband is on the board of directors. Reading the book had a lasting effect on me and has helped me cope with the unexpected changes in my life. Second, it was reading this book that led me to another book: *Streams in the Desert* by L. B. Cowan.

I cannot recall how I got to know about the book, but I went ahead and purchased a copy. Years before, I'd seen an interview by Pastor Mark Finley with Joni on the televised program, *It is Written*. There she shared her story about her life and her disability. At the time of the interview, I wasn't a part of the disability population, but I was so captivated when I saw how she'd turned her pain into something beautiful for the Lord. She'd dedicated her life in helping others within the disability community to move beyond their limitations and to become productive individuals in the society in which they lived. After watching the broadcast, without hesitation, I purchased the video and watched it again.

Apart from the Bible, every day I'd read *Streams in the Desert*. This book became an anchor for my soul. It was in sync with the Word of God. The daily readings were right on point. I gained so much blessings from this little devotional that I went back online and purchased several copies in bulk and gave them as gifts to other women. The feedback was great!

Books added to my everyday reads were *You'll Get Through This: God's Story Your Story* by Max Lucado, *Knowing God's Will for Your Life* by Dr. Charles Stanley, *Wounded Women of the Bible* by Dena Dyer & Tina Samples, *Gray Matter* by David Levy MD with Joel Kilpatrick, and *Brain Health: How to handle your head,* by Sharon Platt-McDonald. Also included were the daily lesson study and morning watch reads.

I was also fortunate to receive devotional books from some of my sisters in Christ. *Jesus Calling* by Sarah Young, the *Word for Today—Caribbean Edition*, supplied to me quarterly by my sister living in Jamaica, and *Daily Bread*, the yearly edition given to me by my mother. Each author offered me something that helped me build my faith, hope, and trust in God and took me through each day. It was a daily, intentional walk with God. However, the Bible was the number one book coupled with prayers, whether I prayed aloud or silently and of course journaling. These were the main activities of any given day.

Who was Gabby Gifford? Well, Gabby Gifford, was a former congresswoman from Arizona. She was shot and severely wounded in her head at a mass shooting during one of her political rallies in January 2011. It was an assassination attempt on her, the exact year I experienced the brain (cerebellar) aneurysm. Her situation was a matter of life and death, just like mine. The chances of her surviving looked grim, just like mine. The only difference between us was she was shot in the head and I had a cerebral aneurysm. I could relate to Gabby's story when I read it. We both experienced severe brain injuries.

Gabby, after her brain injury, like me, had difficulty speaking, walking and losing her independence. After intensive speech and physical therapy programs, she eventually spoke and walked again and regained her independence. I on the other hand was able to speak and walk again, but didn't regain my full independence. Although I was able to walk again, I still needed a cane to assist me with gait and mobility issues and had to confront residual effects that affected my expressive and receptive language skills. Throughout Gabby's ordeal, Mark, her husband became her stabilizing force. For me, Wendell, my husband also filled that role. Like Joni and Ken, after her injury Gabby and her husband Mark Kelly, a retired astronaut, became co-founders for the advocacy group *Americans for Responsible Solutions.*

Joni Erickson-Tada, Gabby Gifford, and I all had something in common. We had sustained injuries that changed our lives forever. However, despite the severe injuries, reading the stories of these two women helped me to persevere, to be resilient, and showed that I could overcome the odds just like they did despite their injuries and disabilities. Both women, despite their severe injuries, are still living productive lives. And from both their stories, I also learned that I too could live a productive life after a traumatic experience. Life still continued for them, and it certainly could continue for me.

From Sharon Platt-McDonald's book, *A Sound Mind: Thinking Your Way to Vibrant Health*, I learned about what it would take to have a sound mind. As I read the book, it was then that I learned the importance of being thankful despite my challenges. Praising God became very therapeutic for me. It played a major role in my recovery. There were several times when I felt I was going under emotionally, or I felt spiritually and emotionally drained. And at times I also felt lonely. But it was praising God through scriptural songs, prayers, and the stories and promises in the Bible that kept me, so I wouldn't let go. Praising God helped me to keep my focus on Him instead of myself. It was in the darkest of moments that my hope and strength were renewed, my joy returned, and my trust in God restored.

The psalmist David declared, "He bought me up also out of an horrible pit, out of the miry clay, and set my feet upon a rock, and established my goings. And he hath put a new song in my mouth, even praise unto our God: many shall see it, and fear, and shall trust in the Lord" (Ps. 40:2–3, KJV). Like David, this is how I felt in times of despondency and fear; then Jesus came and made the difference when I praised Him.

I also found out that having a grateful heart in trials and sufferings boosted my mental health. And that was good to know. When I looked back on where my journey began to the present, I'd so much to thank my heavenly Father for. I was undeserving, but regardless of how undeserving I felt, He showed me through the people around me and the daily miracles that He loved me immensely. And all I could do was to express my thankfulness to Him each day.

Attitude! Attitude! Attitude! I'd to make some serious lifestyle changes, as in: "In quietness and confidence shall be your strength" (Isa. 30:15, KJV). Prayer was also a very important element of the healing process. It helped to keep my stress level down and to maintain peace of my mind. Having a positive attitude helped me also to keep my hope alive and led me to believe that one day in the distant future, the sun would shine for me again.

Another nugget I picked up as I neared the end of the book was, I should value who I was. Just reading that statement from the author, Sharon Platt-McDonald, brought encouragement to my soul. Here, I was feeling emotionally bruised and broken, and the next chapter I was about to read was entitled "Value Who You Are". The chapter began with "Ye have not chosen me, but I have chosen you, and ordained you, that ye should go and bring forth fruit" (John 15:16, KJV). Followed by "This scripture creates such a beautiful image of God's love and the value He places on us. It is simply saying that, even when we did not have Him in mind. God still chose us" (Sharon Pratt-McDonald, p. 88). No matter the situation, I was loved and valued by my heavenly Father.

"Even when I walk through the darkest valley, I will not be afraid, for you are close beside me. Your rod and your staff, protect and comfort me" (Ps. 23:4 NLT).

Chapter 11

The Grim Reaper Strikes Twice

My mother's only sister who resided in Jamaica, had been battling a rare form of cancer for some time. She eventually succumbed to it on February 10, 2012. This was just four months since I became ill and was trying to turn the corner in my recovery. My mother, Iris was my caregiver in the daytime, while my husband worked. This was another blow for all of us. Now, my mother had to go home to Jamaica to attend her only sister's funeral. At this stage in my recovery, I was still unable to walk. I couldn't stay alone. I needed round-the-clock assistance.

We were in dire straits to find someone who would take up the mantle. It wasn't long that a dear church sister that I referred to as my "church mother" volunteered and stepped in to take care of me in the day in my mother's absence. Problem solved! God showed up just when our backs were against the wall. "Sister D," moved into our home and took care of me. I'll always be grateful to "Sis. D" for endearing herself to me and my family.

Before my mother's departure to Jamaica to funeralize her sister, I'd watched as she grieved in silence over her loss. As a matter of fact, we were all grieving over this great loss. My mother and her sister had a very close relationship, and I knew that she was hurting badly because she was not present to bid her sister goodbye. This was an aunt who had been very loving, caring, and kind to me, someone who I'd a close relationship with from my childhood. And here I was in no shape to go with my mother to attend her funeral. That made it even more difficult for me. My mother attended her sister's funeral in Jamaica and returned to the US within a week from the day she left. On her return, she resumed her caregiving. God kept us. What a mighty God we serve!

Then on November 30, 2013, the Grim Reaper struck again. This time it was my father. He too had finally lost his battle with prostate cancer. For the second time we were meeting with death. To attend my father's funeral, I'd to get clearance from my neurologist. And secondly, I couldn't travel on my own. To travel, I needed someone to accompany me. By this time, I'd graduated from a walker to a cane. I was now making baby steps, but on traveling to the funeral I'd to use a wheelchair because I was unable to walk long distances on my own.

This was a very emotional time for me. In less than two years I'd lost my father, Louis and my aunt Iona. Before I came home from rehab, my father, Louis was the one who received and assembled my wheelchair and bath chair when both were delivered at my home in December of 2011. This was my father who, along with my mother, acted as my caregivers back then. Here was a man who used tapes to mark the steps on the stairway of my home, assembled my bath chair, installed a hand shower and secured all rugs and carpets for my safety. And now he was no more.

In times when we desperately are in need of God, He shows up and is on time! And this was just another instance of how much He cared. The day after his death, the search for an airline ticket began. A reasonable priced ticket was found and purchased by faith. The problem was, I couldn't travel alone. At the time, it wasn't feasible for my husband to leave at the same time as I did. He would follow in a few days. So, I needed someone to accompany me to Jamaica.

Here comes "Sis D" to the rescue! God provided again! "Behold, I am the LORD, the God of all flesh. Is there anything too hard for Me?" (Jer. 32:27, NKJV). Two days after the airline ticket was purchased, "Sis. D" and I were off to Jamaica. After traveling for three hours and some, we landed on the island where I was born. This time I was returning on a sad occasion. My father was dead!

After I left the airport, my sister's husband Benedict took me to my mother's home. I can recall one day sitting alone in my parent's bedroom, overcome with raw emotions. Here I was, facing my father's burial in a couple days' time. How would I handle the moment? What would be my emotional state? Just at that moment an impression was made on my mind. The Holy Spirit was speaking. I heard Him say, "Do you remember the song the choir sang last Sabbath in church?" Then the title of the song flashed across my mind. In an instance a peace came over me. It was as if I was being told "Be still, and know that I'm God" (Ps. 46:10, KJV)! At that moment I felt the Holy Spirit's presence, and I was receiving the assurance in the quietness of the room that He would sustain me through those painful days and I was never alone.

And the Holy Spirit did do His work in me. From that day on, I knew I was going to be all right because the Holy Spirit told me so, and He used a song to comfort me then. I felt stronger spiritually, emotionally, and physically throughout my father's funeral service. By divine intervention, I made it! Praise God!

"And these stones shall be a memorial to the children of Israel forever" (Josh. 4:7 NKJV).

Chapter 12

Make Me a Memorial and Lesson from Two Fruit Trees

Twelve stones representing the twelve tribes of Israel taken from the River Jordan by the priests were to remind the children of Israel of God's miraculous workings in their lives as they continued their journey to Canaan. The Ark of the Covenant, a symbol of God's presence with them as they traveled to the Promised Land, also reminded me that I too, no matter the circumstance, the physical and spiritual brokenness, I was not alone. God was with me. For me, my stones, my memorials, were several scriptures and inspirational quotes framed on wall hangings, and of course the many journals and anthology of songs I'd accumulated since October 2012. Like the children of God, these were reminders of God's providential care and interventions in my life.

It was a quiet morning. I was sitting in my favorite chair. Then, in the stillness of the room, a voice distinctly said to me "*Make me a memorial.*" I'd come a very long way from October 8, 2011. Now I was able to sit up in a chair, brush my teeth, and feed myself without assistance. And gingerly but bravely, I took steps around the house with the aid of a cane.

My memorials began with scriptures and an anthology of songs that had a strong impression on me and later grew to include at this point many journals. But what else could I have added to complete the memorial? As I sat in my favorite chair, the Holy Spirit said to me, *"Wall hangings of your favorite scriptures and inspirational quotes."* I thought about what I'd heard and headed over to the computer.

It took me a good while to reacquaint myself with the computer, but I did! In the search box, I typed "scriptural wall hangings," and several came up. I searched for the ones that meant a great deal to me and immediately placed my order. By the next week, I received the framed scriptures and later on in the month, I purchased some framed inspirational pieces. I took my time to decide where I was going to hang each. The framed pieces were strategically placed all over my home, in full view for me to see at a glance anytime whether I looked upward or from any direction.

If you came through the front door you'd be greeted by a framed scripture on the wall. Hanging on the wall across from my favorite chair were three more framed scriptures. Whether I sat or walked in my home, I had memorials that reminded me of God's miracles in my life, His sustaining power, and His immeasurable love for me. Through my brokenness I sensed all the time God's presence with me. I was so broken that I'd to find a wall hanging that reminded me of Isaiah 64:8 (KJV): "But now, O Lord, thou art our father; we are the clay, and thou our potter; and we all are the work of thy hand." God was the Potter and I was the piece of clay in His hand. As the piece of clay, I was filled with impurities that weren't becoming for a child of God. I needed to go through the process of His molding and making me so I could be used by Him. And what a process it was! But the same God who placed me on the potter's wheel also reassured me in Jeremiah 29:11, (NKJV) that He had a good future and hope for me. However, the crucibles just kept on coming in the form of illnesses. Each time, the fire got hotter and hotter. But God!

As time marched on, I realized that God was using these fiery trials to fashion me into a vessel of honor to be used by Him to do His biddings and to declare His glory to others. He was God! It was a struggle to submit to the pressure. However, I've always remembered the apostle Paul and his fiery trials (2 Cor. 11:16–27 KJV) and how he eventually became God's masterpiece and mouthpiece. He was used by God to spread the gospel.

There were many times on my journey that I had to rely on this scripture, "Be still, and know that I'm God;" (Ps. 46:10 KJV). On other days, I'd be reminded that "For with God nothing shall be impossible" (Luke 18:27, KJV).This verse became so meaningful to me for good reasons. No one expected me to survive the brain aneurysm, and even if I did, I'd be living the rest of my life in a vegetative state. What doctors thought was impossible was made possible by Sovereign God!

"Though the fig tree does not blossom, Nor fruits on the vines; Though the labor of the olive may fail, And the fields yield no food; Though the flock may cut off from the fold, and there be no heard in the stalls—Yet I will rejoice in the Lord, I will joy in the God of my salvation" (Hab. 3:17, NKJV).

Another favorite window of mine was in my bathroom. From this small window, I'd observed a lesson in nature. Spring turned to summer, fall turned to winter and winter to spring. Winter seemed the longest and the harshest. I eventually began taking tiny steps with the aid of a cane. From this little window, I could see two fruit trees, a pear and a fig tree. In the fall, both trees would gradually shed the leaves that once adorned their branches. I'd watched as the trees stood exposed to the cold, with no sign of life in the winter months. Both trees endured the harshness of the seemingly unending winter, producing no fruits. The trees both appeared dead—no sign of life, no place for the birds to make nests or for squirrels to find food. Then came spring, and both trees began to show signs of life. Spring was a time of rebirth, renewal, restoration, and rejuvenation.

My heavenly Father was using things He created to teach me sound spiritual lessons from a small window in my bathroom. I would watch each spring as the pear tree transformed from a lifeless tree to a tree laden with beautiful white blossoms.

Then within a few more weeks, the beautiful, pristine flowers would change into tiny pears and the tree would once again be covered with green leaves. The tiny pears would eventually mature into delicious fruits. A sign of life again.

The fig tree also stood in the harsh winter with its branches looking dry and fragile. But here comes spring. In the middle of the new season came, a rebirth, a newness of life. Tiny leaves began to sprout from the root of the fig tree. And within three weeks the fig tree that stood lifeless was covered all over with green leaves, followed by figs.

Just watching these trees gave me renewed hope. They assured me that all was not lost. God didn't abandon me. I compared my life to the life of those two fruit trees. At first, the trees appeared dead and lifeless. Then the seasons changed, and there was life again. I went through a dark period in my life that I called the cold and harshness of my existence—my winter. I'd made improvements, and that felt like springtime to me. My brokenness, hurt, and pain were finally replaced with joy. "Weeping may endure for a night, But joy comes in the morning" (Ps. 30:5, NKJV). I felt a rebirth in spirit and purpose.

My vision of seeing myself whole again spiritually and physically was on its way. Habakkuk 2:3 NKV became clearer and clearer to me. "For the vision is yet for an appointed time; But at the end it will speak, and it will not lie. Though it tarries, wait for it; Because it will surely come, it will not tarry." God would certainly restore. But I'd to patiently wait. All was not lost. So, like the apostle Paul, I "Rejoicing in hope; patient in tribulation; continuing instant in praying" (Rom. 12:12 KJV). I believed that one day I'd be made completely whole again. Looking forward to it! Thank you Jesus.

And He said unto me, My grace is sufficient for thee: for my strength is made perfect in weakness. Most gladly therefore will I rather glory in my infirmities, that the power of Christ may rest upon me" (2 Cor. 12:9, KJV).

Chapter 13

MY LIFE TODAY

Prayer, the Bible, journaling, religious music, family, friends, strangers and my community of faith have all remained parts of the ecosystem of my existence and can never be forgotten. Because those were the sources that I relied on to keep my faith anchored in God. The trajectory of my life continues to be in the hand of my Creator, Sustainer, Redeemer Promise-keeper and Friend. And I thank God for gifting me with an unbreakable spirit.

Two significant dates during my recovery were recorded by Sister Primrose, a member of my faith community. She kept dates in her Bible of the first and second times when I returned to corporate worship, June 23, 2012 and August 18, 2012.

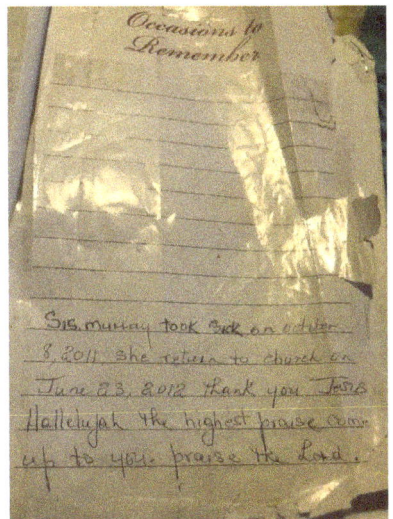

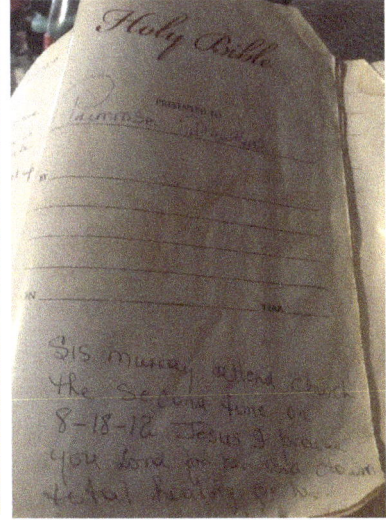

The issue was how long could I stay? What time would I leave? Those were questions I had to deal with because I feared going back to corporate worship. I believed then that I would have to relive the experience of Sabbath, October 8, 2011 just by going back into the Sanctuary.

However, I was warmly welcomed back into fellowship. Remember Dr. Kadien, the physical therapist, a member of my church who did extra therapy sessions with me? Well, she accompanied me on my first Sabbath back to church. Her presence made the experience a stress-free one. I gradually immersed myself back into corporate worship. But there are still times when I experience weird nauseous spells that will engulf my head. And I will have to seek immediate medical attention.

The brain aneurysm has left me with several visible and invisible issues. I've accepted the changes in my life, and I try each day to develop more coping skills and strategies to camouflage my deficits. I still struggle with my gait and balance, which result in staggering and unsteady walking. I'm still dependent on a cane to assist me when I walk.

Today, balancing on either leg is still a challenge. And going up and down a flight of stairs without holding on to the rails for extra support is also a daily occurrence. Stepping into a pair of pants, dress, or skirt is difficult for me to do. This was once a simple activity for me, but these days I can't complete the action without some form of support as an aid. However, I thank my God that I'm still able to move around at my own pace.

Twenty-plus years have passed, since my retina and lens implant surgeries and my experience with blindness in my right eye. Since then I've faced two surgeries on the left eye. Now, I'm dealing with glaucoma and frequent four months visits to the eye specialist have become a part of my existence. During one of my visits, it was discovered that a thin "film" that looked like a piece of saran wrap had grown over the lens implant in my right eye.

The "film" obscures my sight; and it is not guaranteed that there will be any improvement, even if I should undergo another surgery to have it remove. Due to all these issues with my eyes, I've lost the ability to see details. As a result of the damage of the optic nerve in the right eye, it has lost its ability to produce tears. These days most of the seeing and crying is done by the left eye. I continue to hear only with my left ear because the hearing in my right ear hasn't returned.

As was described in a previous chapter, the 'freezing' sensation on the right side of my face is constant. Sometimes it feels like an army of ants running up and down under the skin. It was during my time in rehabilitation I felt the change. I thought it would go away with time. I would just have to wait. "Wait on the Lord; be of good courage, And He shall strengthen your hand; wait, I say, on the Lord" (Ps. 27:14 NKJV)!

It's now ten years and counting and the 'freezing,' ticklish sensation has remained. It begins from my forehead and extends to the lower right corner of my mouth. And it also affects my right nostril, preventing me from breathing properly and pulls on my right eye, affecting my vision. The only time I do not experience these feelings is when I'm asleep. The moment my eyes are opened, the tingling and numbness begin all over again. And if I should be stuck with a sharp instrument on the same side, the feeling is totally different from the left side. What I originally called "my invisible hell" I now refer to as "my thorn in the flesh". To this day, the issues regarding my vision and mouth are still on going and there are times when my lips would balloon.

Like Paul the Apostle, I too have said many prayers, asking God to remove the discomfort but I'm always reminded "My grace is sufficient for you, for My strength is made perfect in weakness" (2 Cor. 12:8, NKJV). Living on divine grace and God's promises is how I live my life today. Because I never know what a second, a minute, an hour or a day will bring. Whenever the nauseous feeling rears its ugly head, I can't take any chances. As the psalmist David said: "I shall not die, but live, And declare the works of the Lord" (Ps. 118:17, NKJV).

At nights, I wear a patch over the right eye because it's unable to close on its own when I'm asleep. Laying on the right side of my head is very uncomfortable and lowering my head causes a nauseous feeling. This has resulted in me having to be in the care of three eye and dental specialists along with the neurologist.

Due to the aneurysm, the right section of my scalp remains numb. There are instances when that section of my head itches, and I have difficulty locating the area of discomfort. So, I usually comb the base of my head in the lower right corner next to my ear to help me identify the area or run my fingers through my hair. The comb would send signals that would eventually soothe the area. On any given morning, the first thing to greet me, when I wake, is excruciating pain in both eyes. The pain will continue for some time until an eye lubricant is applied and then it will slowly disappear. And each day, I'm subjected to taking two prescribed eye drops to treat my glaucoma.

Other times, the area between my right eye and ear will itch uncontrollably. In order to get relief, I will gently stroke the area until the itching stops. I still experience sudden sharp, stinging surges of pain on the right side of my head running from the front to the base of my neck. This has raised a cause for concern. However, I've since discussed the issue with my neurologist, and he told me that's one of the effects from the aneurysm.

I still have issues with, physical and mental fatigue. It doesn't take much for me to get tired and feel fatigued. I always have to keep in mind my limitations and when to call it quits. Transitioning from the indoors to outdoors can be a challenge at times.

Sometimes, I'm still plagued with numbness in my left arm, hand, fingers, left foot and toes. Over time, I've adjusted to the loss of hearing in my right ear. This has impeded my receptive and expressive language skills, resulting in my inability to hear correctly what has been spoken. As a former learning disabilities teacher, I've since incorporated coping skills and learning strategies to help me function daily.

Regarding my speech, while in a conversation, my voice will sometimes transition from an adult to a childlike voice and vice versa. The pitch and tone have also been affected. When speaking in public, I pray silently that my voice will not change because I'm often embarrass having to explain myself to my listeners.

Using words sometimes in the proper context has been challenging for me. Case in point, instead of saying "I'm going to the kitchen" I'll end up saying "I'm going to the chicken." Instead of saying, "There's light at the end of the tunnel" I'll say "There's light at the end of the towel" or "There's life at the end of the tunnel."

In order to deal with my speech and long term memory deficits, I have to depend on strategies like mnemonics and use letters of the alphabet to find words and use them in correct sequence and context when expressing myself. Sometimes it takes a little while to put my thoughts together in order to make what I'm saying make sense verbally and to be understood in the written form.

It has been a long time since I've enjoyed the different tastes of food. My taste buds are no longer functional. What should be sour is now sweet, and what should be sweet is now sour. Eating is still a chore because of the way I chew food and I still have to use a spoon to deposit the food properly into my mouth.

When the barometric pressure is about to change, it affects the right side of my face including the corner of my lips. Whenever there is a stressful situation and a climate of negativity, I literally divorce myself from it and I have to make sure that I constantly keep a check and record readings of my blood pressure. I still have to make yearly visits to the neurologist for checkups.

The acronym FAST has become an indelible part of my life. It is always a race against time! These days I don't have to be concerned with my right hand using objects as weapons. Due to positive self-talk, telling my right hand not to throw objects, I've overcome this issue.

There are still days when I experience very, very low moments. One morning in particular, while watching a religious broadcast, an overwhelming feeling swallowed me up. It was so bad that I just wanted to die. I immediately closed my eyes and began to pray about the matter. It was then that I heard from the device in my lap, the speaker uttering loud and clear: "My strength is made perfect in weakness," which was followed by a song about God's grace and mercy. Right then and there, I knew the Holy Spirit was speaking to me, reassuring me that I had to solely depend on God to get me through moments like those and not on myself.

Not too long ago, I was in the backyard when I heard a crackling sound from my left ear. The sound got my attention, and when I turned to look, I was just in time to see an iron pole coming towards me. The minute I sensed what was going to happen, I automatically switched to a fright and flight mode. I'd forgotten that running was a thing of the past.

I managed to make two steps from the impending danger and fell on my wrist. At first, I thought my wrist was broken, due to the excruciating pain and the sudden swelling. The same day, I was fortunate to have Dr. Hopeton, a nurse practitioner from my community of faith look at it. I thank God my wrist was not broken but instead, I suffered a sprain. Due to the injury (by the way it was my left hand, my dominant hand), I couldn't use my hand for two weeks.

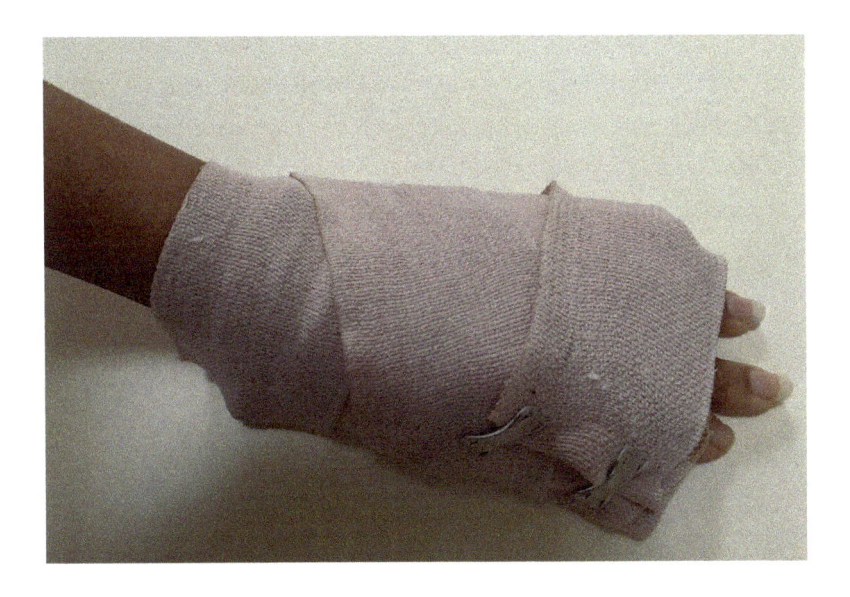

These days, I make sure that each day I intentionally spend time with God. This has become a huge part in my life. A time when I read the Bible, pray, or focus on a religious song or article and its implication on my life as a disciple of Christ. God's promises have become my mantra and one of the songs that is always at the forefront of my mind is "Standing on the Promises of God," in particular verse two:

<u>Standing on the Promises of God</u>
Standing on the promises that cannot fail,
When the howling storms of doubt and fear assail,
By the living Word of God I shall prevail,

Standing on the promises of God.

*Author Russell Kelso Carter (1886)
Copyright Public Domain*

There's a narrative in the New Testament that resonates with me. And it's the narrative of the woman with the issue of blood. For twelve years, she was plagued with a serious health issue until she met Jesus. The moment Jesus stepped in her space, her life was transformed both physically and spiritually. Although she was in a crowd, Jesus knew that someone had touched Him and with compassion and empathy made her whole again. I could say the same! The apostle Paul also reminds us that "We are hard-pressed on every side, yet not crushed; we are perplexed, but not in despair; persecuted, but not forsaken; struck down, but not destroyed" (2 Cor. 4:8 NKJV).

Because of Jesus' love and acceptance of me, I've learned over the years to love and accept myself. I've also learned to see myself with possibilities instead of a person with disabilities. I've refused to allow my physical deficits to define who I am. I've also refused to let others define who I am—because I know Whose I am. I'm a child of God, created in His own image after His likeness! I'm royal! I've chosen to live a happy, healthy, and productive life, doing what I can to promulgate the Gospel.

And when God opens the door for me to share my story, without hesitation, I walk through it. So far, God has been opening doors for me to share my story where I least expect. I've been invited on many occasions to share my story on prayer lines and on a Christian television network, and I'll continue to do so as long as I live. God's name must be glorified! My God is a faithful and amazing God! I praise Him for transforming my life and for loving me the way He does.

My Life Today

My life today is focused on ministries. Unable to move around as I used to, I use my sphere of influence to be involve in ministries. Of which are "*Glasses for Jesus*" and "*Shoes for Men.*" In Glasses for Jesus, I collect used eyeglasses for females and males and donate to a Christian organization. The glasses are cleaned and distributed to people in countries where it's unaffordable for some individuals to purchase eyewear.

My motive for engaging in such a ministry is to give individuals the chance to obtain eyewear to be able to read the Bible and to learn about Jesus. And of course, I'm also motivated by the struggles I have with my sight. I know how it feels when one's vision is impaired and it's a struggle to see and read. I'm presently living this reality. Affordability, is another concern of mine. And I want people who cannot afford to purchase eyewear due to their socioeconomic status to get the gift of sight.

"Shoes for Men" is another project I've done. One hundred new pairs of men's shoes have been collected and sent to a center of influence in another country. This center of influence caters to the poor and homeless in the inner city of that country. The shoes were given to men who had no footwear. Toiletries have also been collected for female and male alike and shipped to the same center of influence for distribution.

Also, clothing and toys have been collected and sent to a country in Africa. Making what looks impossible become possible is how I want to spend the rest of my life. Despite my deficits, I thank God, He has given me a second chance on life. And I deemed it a privilege, I'm ecstatic that I've been given the opportunity to participate in sharing the Gospel with others in tangible and meaningful ways. Regardless of my visible and invisible impairments, I believe I'm still a disciple of Christ and still have much to offer. I have a purpose to fulfill!

I've found so much encouragement and hope in the Promises from the Old to the New Testament, and I'd like others also to "Taste and see that the Lord is good; Blessed is the man who trusts in Him" (Ps. 34:8, NKJV)!

Every day still has it challenge. There are days when I'm in pain and suffer severe discomfort and other days where I'd get a respite. But I take comfort in the fact that my body is just a temporary structure, and one day in the near future I'll exchange a body that is broken for a new one. At the second coming of Jesus, I look forward to the day when these words will become a reality, "For this corruptible must put on incorruption, and this mortal must put on immortality. So when this corruptible has put on incorruption, and this mortal has put on immortality, then shall be brought to pass the saying that is written: "Death is swallowed up in victory." "O Death, where is your sting? O Hades, where is your victory?" (1 Cor. 15:53—55, NKJV).

Due to the suddenness of the brain aneurysm, I've felt short of the time I needed for full retirement. I'd to retire before my expected time, losing out financially. BUT God! Since October, 8, 2011, God has provided in miraculous ways, that I cannot explain. It will never make sense to the human mind. No explanation will do! Over the years, I've maintained and formed new friendships locally and globally on a particular platform of which I'm grateful. Every day I receive words of encouragement from these individuals and they're fully invested in my well-being.

I've truly experienced the meaning of Matt. 6:25 (NKJV): "Therefore I say to you, do not worry about your life, what you will eat or what you will drink, nor about your body, what you will put on. Is not life more than food and the body more than clothing ... For your heavenly Father knows that you need all these things." This promise and the song, "God Will Take Care of You" by Martin

Civilla D., (1904) Public Domain, have always reminded me, that no matter the circumstance, God has promised to take care of me. So, there is no need for me to be anxious or afraid.

In Revelation 4:3, KJV, I read: "And he that sat was to look upon like a jasper and a sardine stone: and there was a rainbow round about the throne, in sight like unto an emerald." Whenever I see a rainbow in the sky it reminds me of God the great Promise Keeper. And I'm also encouraged by the words, "Let us hold fast the confession of our hope without wavering, for He who promised is faithful," (Hebrews 10:25). It gives me great joy just to know that I serve a God that is faithful and He will never go back on His word.

Until then, I'm fully persuaded that Jesus will keep me "He will not crush the weakest reed or put out a flickering candle" (Isa. 42:3 NLT). He'll be with me to the end. And not once did His promises ever fail!

References

Bradshaw, J. (Host). Nedley, N. Dr. (Speaker). (2015). It Is Written Script 1360 [Controlling Your Emotions]. It Is Written International. Chattanooga, TN: Hope Channel.

Bradshaw, J. (Host). Nedley, N. Dr. (Speaker). (2016). It Is Written Script 1365 [Boosting Your Brain]. It Is Written International. Chattanooga, TN: Hope Channel.

Chalmers E. PhD. (1998), Healing the Broken Brain, (United States of America): Remnant Publications, pp. 10, 34, 60–68.

McDonald-Platt, S. (2012), A Sound Mind; Thinking your way to vibrant health, (Europe): Autumn House Publications, pp. 56–128.

Khatri, M., MD., 'Understanding Tinnitus -- the Basics', medically reviewed on November 12 2019, viewed on 18 November 2021, https://www.webmd.com>

Songs

Civilla D. Martin, "*God Will Take Care of You,*" Public Domain, (1904)

Clarke Kelso Russell, "*Standing on the Promises.*" Public Domain, (1886).

Collingsworth Family, Carolyn Adkins, "*Fear Not Tomorrow,*" P&KC MUSIC LLC, September 2010. *(Permission granted)*

Matheson George, "*O Love That Will Not Let Me Go,*" Public Domain, (1882).

Owens J. Priscilla, "*Will Your Anchor Hold,*" Public Domain, (1882).

Bibles Used

All scripture quotations, unless otherwise indicated, are taken from the New King James Version. Copyright 1982 by Thomas Nelson, Inc. Used by permission. All rights reserved.

Scripture quotations marked (KJV) are taken from the King James Version Bible.

Tyndale House Publishers. (2004). Holy Bible New Living Translation (NLT). Wheaton, Ill; Tindale House Publishers

Pictures

Cover photo courtesy of Sherwin Brown (used by permission)

Back cover photo courtesy of Maxine Ranger (used by permission)

About the Author

Marvella L. Murray, graduated from the City University of New York, with a Bachelor of Science Degree in Education (magna cum laude) 1995, concentration on the Emotionally Disturbed. In 2000, she pursued a Master of Science in Education, focusing on Learning Disability.

After completing her studies, Marvella worked in the New York Public School System for several years, as a Resource Room/Special Education Teacher Support Provider, serving the Learning Disabled, Early Intervention and At-Risk populations and as liaison between the school and the School District Office. However, due to a cerebral aneurysm, Marvella retired from teaching on June 14, 2013.

Presently, from her home Marvella spends her time, sharing Jesus through various mediums and finding creative ways to make what seems impossible, possible for herself and others. Using her sphere of influence, she has worked on several successful projects, two of which are *Shoes for Men* and *Glasses for Jesus*.

This book is centered on Marvella's physical and spiritual journey that began on October 8, 2011 and continues even today. In this book you'll read about how God used her physical brokenness to lead her into a deeper and more meaningful relationship with Him, in a time of deep distress.

CPSIA information can be obtained
at www.ICGtesting.com
Printed in the USA
LVHW071645140222
711109LV00020B/759

9 781662 834523